KISMET

A TURKISH-AMERICAN
WOMAN'S UNLIKELY
STORY OF RACE,
LOVE, *and*
PERSONAL
TRANSFORMATION

PALMETTO
PUBLISHING
Charleston, SC
www.PalmettoPublishing.com

Hardcover ISBN: 979-8-8229-3869-4
Paperback ISBN: 979-8-8229-3870-0
eBook ISBN: 979-8-8229-3871-7
Audiobook ISBN: 979-8-8229-3872-4

Cover image is from GÜZELÇAMLI, TURKEY.

To my boys

INTRODUCTION: 911

I could hear the siren at the end of the street. I really hoped it was the paramedics. All I could think of was the baby in my body, and I kept whispering, "Stay with me, baby, stay with me."

My third pregnancy wasn't planned. I badly wanted a girl, but it wasn't to be. We had just moved back from Atlanta, Georgia, and struggled to make ends meet. My ex-husband was the only one working. We could not return to Palo Alto because the rents went up like crazy after we left. We stayed at our friend's house in Oakland and started looking into the more affordable East Bay. We decided on Alameda. It is an island, super close to Oakland, and has a nice downtown. They have older houses that I adored. We rented a duplex with a living room, a kitchen on the top floor, and two small bedrooms in the basement. There was a set of steep hardwood stairs that connected the two floors.

I found out I was pregnant as soon as we moved in. It hit me hard because it didn't seem like a good time to have another child. After my first two boys, I thought this one had to be a girl. Even though my ex wasn't as shocked by the pregnancy as I thought he would be, the following months showed me that there was a severe problem with my marriage. We didn't think about an abortion; if the baby was healthy, we were going to have the baby. I had a very grueling pregnancy, though. My morning sickness was way worse than the first and the second pregnancies. The nausea lasted a whole day, and I didn't know what to eat. I also had debilitating migraines. I could not take anything besides Tylenol, so my headaches would last days. (Finally, the Ob-Gyn prescribed some safe, stronger medication that seemed to help.) I also had a 4-year-old and a 16-month-old to worry about at home. I was home with the 16-month-old most of the day, but thankfully, my 4-year-old had started going to preschool. My ex mostly worked from home.

Around the 16-week mark of my pregnancy, my ex went to New York to teach for a few days. I was alone with the boys. That week, I found out that I was having another healthy boy. I am not going to lie—I was devastated by this news. I was happy he was healthy, but his gender was not what I had hoped for. I was in a haze all week. I went to the library with my 16-month-old for a story hour one day. Leaving the library, I hit another car as I was backing up—a minor accident but one that rattled me.

The following day, I took my 4-year-old to school, returned, and was getting ready to take my 16-month-old to a baby gym class. I prepared my purse and a diaper bag and left it by the door. I had just changed my son's diaper and remembered I had some socks for my son by the stairs. We were about to leave, so I was wearing socks, too. Suddenly, I slipped and fell down the stairs. I somehow managed to land on my right hip—trying to protect the baby—and I crashed down all twelve stairs on my hip. I landed at the bottom of the stairs and sat there in shock. I tried to get up, but it hurt too much to move. I immediately knew something was very wrong.

I told my 16-month-old, who was at the top of the stairs, to get my purse with my cell phone because there was no phone downstairs. But he was too young to understand. He closed the door at the top of the stairs. That lowered my chances of screaming so that the neighbors could hear me. I started thinking about going up the stairs by scooting on my butt. But this seemed like a very painful option. Then, I felt a little trickling down below. I panicked and thought I was about to lose my baby. I felt devastated. A boy or a girl—why would that have mattered? I was about to lose a perfectly healthy child because of my stupidity. Then I remembered there was an iPad on the windowsill right behind me. With my right hand, I grabbed the iPad, which we usually used to play music or bedtime stories for the kids. I remembered that its microphone didn't work, but there *was* a Skype app. I Skyped my mom in Italy. She answered but couldn't hear me, so I sent instant messages through the app. I told her I had fallen and wasn't able to move. My mom started to panic—I could hear it in her voice. I said, "Please get it together and get me help!"

This wasn't a straightforward task: She needed to reach someone in the US so they could call 911 for me. I don't think she could call 911 from Italy, and even if she could, there was no way she could explain herself in English while feeling that panic. She called my sister, but she didn't pick up. She called my ex, but he didn't pick up either. Finally, she called my best friend Banu, who had just given birth a couple of weeks prior. Banu knew something was wrong and picked up right away. My mom told Banu to contact me on Skype.

My son was crying upstairs when Banu reached me, and while I was messaging her, I was also talking to him, trying to console him. Banu asked me for my address and the code for the digital lock on the front door. Not too long after, I heard that siren outside. The paramedics and firefighters came to the door. They knocked and yelled, "Anybody there?" I yelled back: "Come in!" I thought they couldn't hear me, but next thing you know, someone opened the door at the top of the stairs.

They said, "Ma'am?"

I said, "I am here, hurt, and pregnant. Please come and save me!"

He asked, "Is there anybody else in the house?"

I said, "Yes, my 16-month-old son should be upstairs. No one else is at home, and no one can come and pick him up now, so he has to come with us."

The code for the digital lock did not make it to the EMTs. They came into the house through an open window. They came down the stairs and assessed the situation. The stairs were too narrow for a stretcher, so they brought a compact wheelchair and put me on it, and we got outside to the patio. Every time they moved me, I screamed in pain. They finally brought me to the ambulance and strapped my son onto an ambulance seat. We went to the Alameda Hospital, and the doctors took X-rays immediately. The femur's socket, connected to the hip, was broken in three places. I had to be transferred to another hospital because the Alameda Hospital has no maternity ward or OB-GYN. They also said I needed an operation on my hip. Banu's husband and Banu's mom, Dilek, came to the hospital and picked up my youngest son.

Later, my friend Zeynep's husband came to help my son as he cried at night without me. My older son was picked up from preschool by another parent friend, who brought my son to the hospital to see me. I will never forget his face: He started crying when he saw me. Then, my ex-husband finally called me, and I broke down crying, explaining everything to him. That was the first time I cried during the whole incident. I was so focused on getting myself and my son to safety that I did not stop to think about how I felt.

Once I was transferred to another hospital and had surgery, they expected me to start walking immediately. But I could not walk because of the pain. So, they transferred me to yet another hospital for acute physical therapy. I was in so much pain that even with morphine and narcotic painkillers, I still had to ice my hip all the time. My mom flew in from Italy to help my ex with the kids. My youngest son took my absence badly. When they visited me in the hospital, he would ignore me completely. That broke my heart as a mom, but I had nothing else to do but get better. When I came home after two weeks, I could barely walk with a walker and had to use a wheelchair. I stayed upstairs in the living room because I could not go downstairs with a walker. In time, I could switch to crutches with the help of an in-home physical therapist. At this point, we decided to move to a new place with no stairs. My recovery would take a while, and going up and down with the kids would not work.

During this time, my ex's depression became pretty bad. He picked a fight with my mom. He asked me, "Why do you take naps every day?" I couldn't believe this question since I was still trying to recuperate. He really didn't like it when I got sick or weak. Finally, I told him, "You need to go and see a psychiatrist. You need help." He listened and got on antidepressants. My full recovery took years, and I limped for a long time. On the other hand, my ex was good for a while—until one day, he wasn't.

CHAPTER 1:
Me, Myself, and I

I was born in Ankara, Turkey, in May 1977. This city is not as big as Istanbul and is not on the sea, which is one of the things people from Istanbul criticize it about. They might call Ankara a small town, but it's big—it's the capital of Turkey, and I have always liked it. We had a lot of family there, including both my grandmothers and my paternal grandfather.

I was my parents' first child. My dad is a pulmonologist, and my mom is a dentist. Because of these professions, we moved around a lot when I was young, and we left Ankara when I was 3 years old. We would visit almost every winter break and I liked ice skating at Ankara's ice-skating rink. It also snowed there in the winter, unlike Aydın, where I spent most of my childhood. The summers are beautiful in Ankara because it does not get very hot, and you have a cool breeze at night for most of the summer. Public transport works well, and there is a lake right outside the city.

My dad's parents had three girls and a boy, and my grandmother had a couple of miscarriages along the way. They tried hard to have that one boy. They were from the middle of Anatolia but migrated to Ankara to get a better education for their son. It is common in Turkey to strive for a son to carry on the family name. My oldest aunts didn't get a good education and got married early. My youngest aunt was lucky to become a teacher. My mom's parents also migrated from the other side of Turkey to Ankara. My maternal grandfather wanted his daughters to have a good education. My mom was one of the two daughters and a superstar—she finished high school as a valedictorian and got into dental school.

My dad met my mom at the university, where he studied to become a doctor. They dated until they finished their education and got married. They had me very soon after. My mom was only 23 years old, and my dad was 26. They were so young that they didn't understand what it meant to have a child. My mom's mother helped take care of me when my mom went back to work. She doesn't have many fond memories from that time. My dad never helped out with childcare and just distanced himself more and more. Once, my mom found out he was not actually at the hospital when he was "on call," but she ignored this fact for a while.

When I was 3, my dad wanted to go to eastern Turkey to make money as a small-town doctor. My mom didn't want to go but followed him to preserve their marriage. It was such a backward place that my mom's dental practice didn't get any patients because people didn't believe in women dentists. She could only work for the government hospital. My mom never forgave my dad for that move. They stayed in eastern Turkey for about three years. My dad's indiscretions continued in the small town, which my mom continued to ignore. We later left to go to western Turkey to the small town of Aydın when my mom was pregnant with my sister. I went to elementary and middle school in Aydın after my sister was born. I fondly remember this little town where we remained for about ten years. After this decade, my family moved back to Ankara so my sister could pursue her love of music in a conservatory school. She started studying music full-time at ten and eventually became a professional musician.

I have a lot of childhood memories of a place called Güzelçamlı. It is a small village by the Aegean Sea, close to the port town of Kuşadası, where a lot of cruise ships dock. When I was about 6 years old, my dad and his friends built some summer homes. (This is what my dad did as a side hustle for years.) We have had that house for forty years now, and, growing up, I spent all my summers there. My parents would work, so they put the grandparents in charge of watching my sister and me during the week, and then my parents would spend the weekend with us.

Güzelçamlı is my happy place. When I close my eyes and want to go somewhere that is the ultimate place where I am the happiest, I go there. When I was younger, we had a lot of friends that we would hang out with all day at the beach or pool and then meet up later that night to have drinks and hang out by the beach. Once a week, we would go to Tafana, a dance club that played killer tunes so we could dance by the seaside. I had my first boyfriend there and kissed him on the beach for the first time. I still go to this place every other summer with my kids. My kids love it as much as I do, and this place is one last connection with my childhood and my home country since my mom moved away as well.

From a young age, I always had an issue with men. It started with my first sexual experience: When I was 8, I was sexually assaulted by a family member. My mom had just had surgery and was cared for by some family members. He was older than me, probably around 14. I was alone at home as the others were taking care of my mom next door. He came and asked me questions and asked me to lie down with him on the couch. He started touching my vulva. He did it for a while and did not say anything while he was doing it. I knew it was wrong, but I didn't do anything to fight it. I remember not liking it. Before he left, he said, "Don't tell anybody about this." I told my grandma, whose home I stayed at during my mother's surgery. My grandmother confronted him and asked, "What did you do to this girl?" He was quiet, and my grandmother beat the crap out of him with a slipper. I think that stopped him from doing that to me ever again.

I never told my dad—I worried he would lose it. I tried to tell some friends growing up, but who could have understood? I consistently saw this person at family events as the years passed. I acted like nothing happened and tried to forgive him. I always told myself I was the bigger person, so I would let this go. This incident made me worry that I would be raped one day, but thankfully, that never happened.

I could never really let this go until one day, I forgave him after talking to a therapist about trauma. This therapist said that since the family member was very young at the time, he probably was harassed himself or witnessed someone harassing or molesting someone else. This made me look at the incident entirely differently. Once I had empathy for him, it was easier to forgive him. "Forgiveness is giving up all hope for a different past," said Viola Davis in her book *Finding Me*. We cannot change the past, but we can change our outlook on it. I believe that is the best way to deal with trauma.

When I told my mom about my assault ten years later, she said, "Yes honey, it is sad, but this happens to women in Turkey, and a family member had done a similar thing to me."

I come from a country with such a "hush-hush" culture that this was "normal." I do not remember my parents ever talking to me about men or assault. They never told me what to do or not do in a situation like this. When it happened to me, I froze, and then I was ashamed of talking about it, probably because I thought it was my fault. This is a classic victim response. Children in America are brought up in a way that this is part of their education. Our pediatrician even told my kids that she and their parents are the only ones allowed to see their privates. I now hear that the #MeToo movement has reached Turkey. Parents talk to their kids about threats and do not leave them with anybody. In rural Turkey, though, sexual assault is still very prevalent. Virginity is a big deal, and if a woman loses their virginity, they might marry their perpetrator to protect the family's honor.

Another reason why I have trust issues with men is because when I was 11 years old, I found out that my dad was cheating on my mom. Our nanny informed me of this and gave me the gory details. I don't think I knew what sex was, but I was still traumatized by this for a long time. My dad was my favorite parent up to this point in my life, so this was a big loss for me. I had to keep this secret from my mom for many years during the remainder of their marriage. I finally told her when I was 33 when they were getting a divorce. Thinking back, I realize this knowledge was a big responsibility for a little girl.

I told my sister very early on, which traumatized her, too, but I needed an ally dealing with this. She and I always checked my dad's phone and questioned his motives. We constantly warned him not to look at other women. At around age 25 (after living abroad for a while alone), I wanted to face my dad and tell him I knew about his indiscretions. When I told him I knew, he was very calm and non-apologetic. He told me, "This is how men are; get used to it." He also said that I was a feminist. He said, "Gözde, I don't think you should marry or be with someone Turkish. You will not be happy." I listened to him, and he was right about that. The way that Turkish men are brought up is very sexist. They are accepted as the kings of their family. They are very misogynistic and very entitled. Even though I had not gotten the response I wanted from my dad, my relationship with him improved. Coming clean with what I knew somehow released my emotions and trauma. Years later, when I had my first child at 33, my dad said, "Please, Gözde, move to Turkey with your family." He was distraught by the fact that he would not be able to see his grandson regularly. I pretty much said "no."

Around that time, my dad started having an affair with a 21-year-old nurse. My mom finally caught him with the nurse at my parent's house, which triggered their divorce. My dad married the woman when he was 61, and they had a son, my stepbrother, a year later. This means that my stepbrother is one year younger than my oldest son. I was pretty angry about all this and stopped talking to my dad for a while. Today, my stepbrother and my second son are having similar issues with academics and mental health. That led to my father and I bonding again. My dad and the nurse eventually divorced, and he is now back to his old ways of dating multiple women. I tell him not to get married ever again and not to ruin anybody else's life. Surprisingly, he agrees with me.

I can accept him the way he is today, but that doesn't change the fact that his behavior ruined my teenage years—and beyond. I never trusted my boyfriends and picked a husband I thought was the opposite of my dad. My ex was not the cheating kind, but he was emotionally unavailable and moody, just like my dad was.

My parents were young, and I was the first-born, so I grew up quickly. I was always mature for my age, and because of the six-year age gap between me and my sister, Gizem, I felt like a parent to her. She was born in summer 1983. Like me, she is a Gemini, which made my relationship with her much easier. When she was little, she was very spirited, and this made taking care of her challenging. We discovered her talent for music at the age of 2 when I was taking keyboard lessons. My mom took it upon herself to get my sister to a music conservatory. We were still living in Aydın, and my mom convinced my dad to move back to Ankara, where there is a great conservatory. My sister had to go ahead of them and stay with my dad's sister for two years until my mom and dad finally moved to Ankara. My sister was eight then, and being away from my parents greatly affected her psyche. That, and being at a school where people of all ages study music (from elementary school to college), made her grow up quickly. My mom and dad would ask me to accompany her to bars and parties after I was 18. My sister and all her friends looked older than they were and had fake IDs—I was the chaperone in these instances. My parents gave me responsibility for my sister because they could not keep her at home. I was very young and naïve and should not have been given that responsibility.

One New Year's Eve, she said, "Hey, sis, I have a secret that I want to tell you. I am dating a guy who is a lot older than me." She was 13 then, and the man was 21. I could not believe my ears. I couldn't tell my parents because then she would have never trusted me with her secrets again, and I needed that trust so that I could help her. It was a difficult balance. My parents asked me to talk to her and convince her of things, but I had to be careful because I didn't want to lose my sister's trust. Years later, when I was in New York for grad school, I told my sister to come live with me. I wanted her to be independent from my parents and our home country. I felt like she needed to grow up and learn about responsibilities. It was a lot of work, and there was a lot of fighting, but I think it was worth it. I even charged her rent, and she worked at a café her first year in the US since she didn't yet know anybody to help her pursue her music career. My sister ended up doing her doctorate in music and has made herself a great career teaching and performing in NYC. I am very proud of her for all that she has accomplished.

More than 90% of the population in Turkey is Muslim, but Turkey was a very secular country when I was growing up. When you get married, the ceremony must be a civil one if you want the government to recognize it. Former president Mustafa Kemal Atatürk sacrificed himself and saved Turkey when the Ottoman Empire fell apart. He founded the secular republic of Turkey in 1923. Atatürk ensured that education was a big part of the lives of the new generation of men and women in Turkey. My family was pretty secular and modern, and everybody around us was also that way as I grew up. My grandparents were the ones who were religious, and my dad fasted during Ramadan. Other than that, my parents drank alcohol and were totally fine with my sister and I dating. I'm very relaxed about religion because of my upbringing. I believe in God, and when I feel like praying, I pray the way Muslim people pray. I try to be a good person and teach my kids to be the same. I don't dictate my kids' religion and think they can decide what religion they want.

I struggled with school as I daydreamed during most of my classes. I most likely had ADHD (attention deficit and hyperactivity disorder). I liked science and went to boarding school to study science for high school. Even though math was my favorite subject, I went to college for biology. The education system in Turkey is a big reason for that. There is a university entrance test (like the SAT), and your score determines exactly which school and department you go to. I ended up in the Biology Department of Ankara University because my score was not high enough for the Math Department. This was one of the best things that happened to me because I ended up loving biology, especially genetics. I loved and was fascinated by genes inherited from generation to generation. I am always amazed by inherited things, even trauma.

I loved being able to do experiments in the lab. I love how clean and pristine that environment is. The smell of ethanol that we use to sterilize things and the calming sound of a biosafety hood (like the sound of a fan) are the things that come to mind when I think of the lab. The calm and clean nature of the lab is the opposite of how science really works, though. I always tell the young scientists: "Experiments do not work 90-95% of the time, you must learn to be OK with that. If you get disappointed and unhappy every time something does not work, then science is not for you." I am so used to things not working in my profession that it makes me a very optimistic person in my personal life. I am used to things not going my way and get very happy when they do. I do not sit around and sulk about how life has not worked for me. I thank science for that fact.

After my second year of college, I went to England for a summer to learn English. I was 18 at the time, and my mom stayed with me in

London for a week to get me accustomed to my new environment. I ended up taking a year off from my biology degree to stay in England to further improve my English. I lived with an English family and worked as their au pair, an experience that changed my outlook on life beyond my sheltered life in Turkey. An au pair is a person who moves to another country and lives with a family that has kids. The family gives the au pair room and board and some pocket money. In exchange, the au pair takes care of the kids and helps with chores around the house. I also worked in a hotel as a maid and a coffee shop as a waitress to save some money. These are things I would have never done in my home country because I come from privilege. These experiences opened my eyes to new ideas about making money and making my own decisions. When I got back to Turkey, all I could think about was finishing my degree and possibly going abroad for grad school to become a scientist. It took me another five years to be able to achieve that goal. I was accepted to NYU for a PhD program in developmental genetics in 2002, so I moved to New York.

When I was about 15 years old, I told my family and friends that I would marry a Black man and have five multiracial kids. I don't know why I said that, but I just had a feeling about it. Let me paint you a picture: I used to live in a country that had almost no Black people. But I've still always admired Black culture.

At a concert, I met an African American musician (I'll call him "D.") in Ankara. I was 23 then, and he was about five years older. He was the drummer of a Turkish-American jazz band. We hit it off immediately and saw each other three times in different cities before he left for New York. We dated for about six months long distance with emails and Skype calls. I was finishing my master's degree in Turkey but had planned to go to the US for a Ph.D. When I met him, I didn't have any cities in mind where I would study for my PhD, so I picked New York City. I got to the city and moved in with him right away. D. had a 5-year-old son with a woman who was semi-famous. She was a model and an ambassador who spoke out against female genital mutilation. When we met, he had been separated from her for a while, and they were sharing custody of their child. D. was not very fond of his ex and said that she had alcohol abuse issues, but the court didn't have enough evidence to take the child from her. Shortly after I arrived in New York, his ex moved to England after 9/11, and D. was not happy that he couldn't see his son anymore. On one of her visits to New York following her move, she brought D.'s son. I had an opportunity to meet him, and he even stayed with us for a while. The son was a very sweet boy and loved his dad very much.

Five years after my breakup with D., I married a Black man. We were together for sixteen years and married for twelve of those. We have three boys, plus his nephew, who came to live with us for several years (who I accept as my son, too). All told, I came close to raising five kids, all of whom are Black.

I met my ex-husband in December 2004 at a party at Rockefeller University. I was working on my PhD at NYU and had been there for a little over two years. I went to the party with a group of friends from school. They failed to tell me that the party was thrown by a scientist, a biologist, like me. I saw my ex-husband across the room. He was tall and handsome and immediately caught my eye. I just stared at him for a long time until he came and talked to me. He told me he had studied biology and worked in a lab upstate New York.

I told him, "What a coincidence, I am a biologist as well."

He said, "This is a party of biologists, so not really a coincidence."

I had no idea.

We danced for a bit; I was sure he was much younger than me. He showed me his ID, and he was only three years younger. He took my email address and left the party. Three days later, he emailed me and asked to meet for coffee at a Starbucks in Union Square. I was super excited—I really had a feeling about this guy, and I do trust my feelings when it comes to love. I showed up at Starbucks and waited for 45 minutes, but he never showed up. When I went back to meet my friends, one of them told me that there were two Starbucks in Union Square. I knew then that he went to the other one. That night, I e-mailed him and said that I was giving him the benefit of the doubt, that I thought he probably showed up at the other Starbucks, and that we should try again! I gave him my number and told him I would email him in three weeks after I came back from Turkey for winter break. In Turkey, I remember thinking about him and being excited to see him. After returning, I emailed him and asked if he wanted to meet. We wrote down the exact address of the Starbucks we would meet.

We finally met one evening. He was sitting at a table already, and I wanted to get a drink. He didn't even ask me what I wanted. I asked him what he wanted, but he said, "I don't want anything. I don't drink coffee." It was odd that he did not want to get me coffee. But I got myself one and sat with him. He was a little distant and edgy. I asked him questions, but he was very guarded in answering them. He was not like that when I met him at the party—he was very fun then. After we talked a little, I was annoyed. We walked out of Starbucks, and I said goodbye and shook his hand. I was so disappointed that I didn't even want to hug when we went our separate ways.

In about two days, he emailed me apologizing for his behavior. He said he was trying to act cool and was a little nervous. I like giving people second chances—I think it is only fair. I asked him to call me and asked him if he wanted a second chance because his email did not say that. He was a little surprised and said, "Yes, I want a second chance."

We set up a date and met up at the National History Museum. He brought his long-time best friend, a Greek American, who introduced him to Greek and Turkish culture. I brought my best friend from NYU. We all had a really good time at the museum. After a few hours, our friends left, and we went to a sushi restaurant near NYU. We ate our sushi, and then he walked me to the subway station. He asked me for a hug before we said goodbye. It was a good date! For our next date, there was a blizzard in NYC. I texted him before and asked if he was still coming. He was coming from New Jersey on a bus, and I was sure it would be canceled, but he said he was still coming. We met up near NYU again and went to a movie. He told me about "Jungle Fever"—the Spike Lee Movie *Jungle Fever* is about a love affair between a Black man and a white woman back in the 1990s. We held hands while watching the movie.

I asked him to come and stay with me at my apartment in Brooklyn and wait for the blizzard to calm down. He kissed me for the first time at the subway station while waiting for the train. When we got home, I made him some pasta, and he stayed the next nine days with me. He returned to his apartment to get some clothes but returned the same day. He figured out a way to get to work from my place. It took him about 1.5 hours to get to work each way. He didn't care, we were in love.

We continued living together for the next six months. He would return to his apartment for a day and run back to me the next day. Finally, we talked about moving in together. We were practically doing that anyway. I may have pushed him a little, but it just didn't make sense to pay rent in two places, and it just sounded so romantic to live together. We had talked about him going to grad school, and I pushed him to apply. It was one of the first things he told me he wanted to do, so being in grad school myself, I encouraged him. While discussing moving in together, I told him I wanted him to stay in the New York area. I didn't want him to go anywhere else. I think, at that point, his boss was telling him to apply to Stanford because he was an alum. The night before my ex-husband was supposed to move in with me, he changed his mind. I think there were a lot of factors that contributed to that, but mainly, he was scared.

When he told me his decision, I lost it. I think he saw me like that for the first time. I was crying and yelling at him all night. He got really scared, and the next thing you know, he broke up with me. I never forget how painful that was. For the next two weeks, I cried my eyes out and mourned. One of my close friends told me that I should talk to him. I wrote him an email pretty much begging him to come back to me. I said I would never try to change his decisions about his future. He could go wherever he wanted to go for grad school. We would take things one day at a time because I didn't want to lose him.

We met up at Central Park to talk, and he told me he missed me, and we started seeing each other again. We did take it slow for a couple of weeks, and then one day, he just moved in with me. He lived with me for another year and then left for Stanford University for his PhD. I was proud of him for getting accepted, but of course, I did not want him to go. He left, and we had a long-distance relationship for about two years. There were ups and downs about it, but we loved each other and continued doing it. The plan was for me to finish NYU and apply for postdoctoral studies somewhere in the San Francisco area so we could be together. I told him if I was going to move across the country and leave beloved New York City for him, there had to be some kind of commitment. He thought about it for a while and got me a ring, so we got engaged. The following summer, we went to Turkey. He met my parents and my family. We even had an engagement party where some friends and some extended family came. In November 2007, we got married at the courthouse in Santa Clara, CA. The following May, we had a huge wedding reception in Turkey. My ex-husband's mom, dad, and sister, along with ten friends from the US, came.

There were more than two hundred people at the wedding.

The night before the wedding, there is something called a "henna night." My grandmother (my mom's mother) collapsed while she was leaving the henna night. I heard the commotion and ran to the door. All I could see was my sister doing CPR on my grandmother. I shrieked and asked, "What is going on?"

Apparently, she was having a heart attack. I sat beside her and could see that she was gone. It was the first time that I saw a dead person. Her eyes were open but lifeless. Her mouth was curved as if someone had sucked the air from her face. I was sobbing very loudly and saying things like, "My poor grandma, she could not see me getting married."

Then, I called my ex's name and told him to come and say goodbye to my grandmother.

I looked up and saw my mom quietly sobbing. She was the person who lost the most on that night. I went and gave her a hug. When I had arrived from the US ten days prior, I saw my grandmother. She kept telling me that she was not going to make it to my wedding. She somehow knew. I am glad that she made it to the henna night because that was almost like a small wedding.

After everyone left, I told my mom we should postpone the wedding. She said she didn't want to do that as we had all these guests that were from the US on a timeline. The only thing she wanted was to bury her mom before the wedding. Muslims don't believe in making the dead person wait. In a record time, my family set up a funeral, a burial, and a prayer service. I went straight from the graveyard to the hairdresser before the wedding. My sister did my makeup as we had to cancel the makeup artist. The wedding turned out fine; we even danced. When I look at those wedding pictures, I can see my mom's sad face trying to smile. Whenever I tell someone about all this, they often say that maybe this was a bad sign for my marriage.

After the wedding, we went to Cappadocia with some of our guests, which was a lot of fun. Then, everyone left, and my ex and I went on a short honeymoon cruise to the Greek islands. It was only four days because I had to defend my thesis in New York. We saw Santorini, Mykonos, and even Athens. Being on the water was very nice since I love the water so much. The food and the entertainment were also great.

When we got back to the US, I defended my thesis and finished up at NYU. We moved to California and found a two-bedroom apartment in Palo Alto, near downtown. We got bikes and commuted to Stanford on our bikes every day. I started my postdoc at Stanford and tried to adjust to what felt like a cut-throat culture. My ex-husband was already a third-year grad student at Stanford, and sometimes we would meet for lunch. I didn't make many friends at first but then I started a happy hour at a local bar on Fridays with my fellow post-docs. I would send out an e-mail every Friday to tell people where we would meet and what time. I got to meet a lot of international post-docs like me. I made friends who also helped my ex-husband because he had been struggling to find friends for two years. I also became part of Turkish Folk Dance group called "Yöre"(founded by Mehpare Aşkın), my ex also joined the group. He was the only Black member of the group, and everyone loved that fact. I danced all through my first pregnancy until 9 months pregnant. The week I did not go to practice, I had my first son.

These new friends and social outlets were great for me as I was having a hard time in Palo Alto after living in New York. It was a little too quiet for me. My ex-husband would tell me that Palo Alto was also a little too white and elitist. He said people looked at him funny and did not trust him. He felt like they were always questioning his presence. It felt so odd to me that this would be the case. He would say, "This is the reality of the US, Gözde, get used to it!" He had come from an urbanized Atlanta that was heavily segregated. He went from almost all-Black schools to Syracuse University in upstate New York, which was pretty white. He said people would cross the street when they saw him in Syracuse. My ex-husband also met a lot of good friends who were white, and he continues those friendships to this day.

After college, he followed one of those friends to New York where he'd met me. I don't remember him encountering anything bad in New York, but, then again, the city is known as a melting pot. I remember in some neighborhoods; we got looks from Black people as we were an interracial couple. (Mostly Black women would give us those looks.) All these years later, I now understand why that is and totally agree with them (I will come to that later in this chapter).

After two years in Palo Alto, my ex-husband's nephew, who was 10 then, came out from Atlanta and moved in with us. The boy's mom was dealing with a lot of stuff mentally and financially and just gave birth to a new baby. My ex-husband's brothers had already taken care of his nephew, and it was his turn. To be honest, I was in favor of this because I thought his nephew could get a good education in Palo Alto. I pushed for this to happen, but I had no idea how difficult it would be to take care of a child and how my ex-husband would take all this. We brought his nephew to Palo Alto right after Christmas break in 2010. We put him in our local elementary school in Palo Alto to finish 5th grade. The school was mostly white, and with him coming from all Black neighborhoods and schools, I am sure it was quite a culture shock for him. He handled it well, though, and was very popular with the kids—he even got a girlfriend. We hadn't had our kids yet at this point, so it was very hard to have a 10-year-old living with us, especially for my ex-husband. He was doing most of the heavy lifting, talking to the teachers, picking him up from school, and driving his nephew to after-school programs. As time passed, my ex-husband got increasingly depressed and was very upset all the time. He said: "I did everything right until now and ended up caring for my sister's kid." We continued this for two years, but it got so bad that we had to send his nephew back home. At this point, we had just our own first baby, but if I hadn't pushed my ex-husband to make that decision, our marriage was not going to survive. At the time, I thought my ex-husband surely felt this way because his nephew was not his kid. Thinking back, I just delayed the inevitable. Ultimately, I believe he began to feel similarly about our kids.

Our first son K. was born in the spring of 2011. I will never forget the day. I was still in the postdoc program at Stanford and worked until the minute I went into labor. My mom was set to come the next day from Turkey. She really wanted to be in the delivery room with me for the birth. I had gone to the lab that day feeling really tired after a weekend of preparing a new bed and a sleeping space for my mom and the baby. Our nephew was still living with us in our two-bedroom apartment. So, I sat down at my desk in the lab and talked to my bestie and colleague Banu. Suddenly, I felt this trickle that seemed to be coming at a pretty fast rate. I told Banu I needed to go to the bathroom, and she needed to follow me. I went to the bathroom and sat on the toilet, and the trickle kept coming. I knew at this point that my water had broken. Banu called my ex-husband, and we went home, and because I wasn't having any contractions, the hospital told us to wait at home.

My ex-husband set up some towels and plastic trash bags, and I sat on the couch. We watched movies, and our friends Zeynep and Robert came and picked up our nephew to spend the next couple of days with them. We hung out for hours as my trickling continued. At around 3 a.m., we went to the hospital because my contractions were getting closer to each other—almost every 5 minutes. When we got to the hospital, they checked me and said that I was only 1 cm dilated. I could not believe it. For the next 8 hours, my contractions continued to get closer and more painful. I was thinking about natural birth all the way at this point—silly me. At around 11 a.m., they told me that I was still only about 3 cm. They told me that they had to induce me. If the baby did not come after 24 hours of my water breaking, they had to do multiple tests, including a spinal tap, because they would worry about infection. At that point, I had to make the choice of getting induced. They told me it would get even more painful when they induced me. I asked for an epidural along with the induction. Everything went smoothly after that. My pain was gone, and I was able to relax. K. came 29 hours after my water broke— thankfully, no tests had to be done.

My second son D. was born almost three years after my first son. I remember my ex-husband said that my son was lucky not to look Black in America. He had the lightest skin of all of them when he was born. He looks mostly like a Latino or more Mediterranean today. I felt this was such a sad thing for a father to say. D's skin is way lighter, but his build looks a lot like my ex-husband's. I think because of that and D's mental issues, my ex-husband had a complicated relationship with D.

My youngest son A. was born two-and-a-half years after my middle son. He was a surprise, but nevertheless, we loved him very much. He is the darkest of all of them, and my mother-in-law called him the actual Black child of the group. It is unfortunate, but there is colorism among the Black community. According to what I heard from my ex's family, there is a brown bag test that men do when choosing a partner. If a woman is darker than a brown paper bag, they are not worthy of dating. These date back to the time of slavery when the slave owners tried to pick lighter-colored Blacks to work at their homes while the darker-colored Blacks worked in the fields. Friends from more liberal places like California say that this phenomenon happens only in places like the South.

When my ex told me that we should have "the talk" with our boys about police and racist people so that they could always be on guard, I was shocked!

"How could this be? This will traumatize the kids," I said.

He told me that it is better than being dead! When you think of it like that, yes, it makes sense. When my ex had gone ahead and told our firstborn K. (9-years-old at the time) during our separation that he needed to be careful with the police, and they might kill him because of the color of his skin, I was livid. Because I never believed that this was a conversation to have that early. I think that the trauma of growing up thinking that the police would kill you is frightening. I experienced that with my ex. As he got older, he became more depressed and affected by his trauma. I thought there was very little control that Black people had regarding the police. If the police were going to kill them, it was just going to happen. But growing up with that trauma is worse, especially if you find out early. I had already told him about my opinion and told him that if he was going to traumatize the kids, he should leave the talking to me. One day, he decided that it was the day to talk to K. I will never forget how my son told me about this. He said that his dad had told him the police would kill him because he is Black. He started crying. My heart fell into a million pieces. This is a great example of how you can't protect your child in your home. I told my ex that it was unfair that he had this talk without me. His response was, "You are not Black. You would not understand."

When I found out that my ex had a girlfriend during our divorce process, I was shattered. I had weeks and weeks of feeling guilty about moving on and feeling happier. I felt stupid when I realized that my ex already had a girlfriend. Also, the realization that his girlfriend was Black hit me hard. I had known that my ex never dated a Black woman before me, and I had found that very strange. His moving on with a Black woman right after me made me feel like I was a transitional woman. Was I the person who made him realize he needed to be with a Black woman? What did I do? Was it all the stuff going on after Trump was elected that made him do this? I will never know. This was another thing that I had to get over.

I have always had a very high respect for Black women. We lived in Atlanta for seven months, and I got very close with my ex-husband's family and friends, especially the women. Some are single mothers because the fathers were not around for various reasons.

Those men were either in prison or with other women or didn't want to be fathers at all. These beautiful, strong, educated Black women had a very small pool of men that they thought they could date or marry. They would endure so much just to be with these guys. If those guys went for women who are not Black, the women would lose out on that potential pool of eligible Black men. I understand that so well now. Having gone through a marriage with a Black man and seeing how complicated their lives are living in the US, I think it makes sense. I also don't think Black men are completely OK with being with other races, especially white women. In both of my relationships, I was told I was not white. I mean, I could be "white-passing" because of the way I look, but I am from another country and not Christian. I know a lot of Turkish people who identify as white. We are Caucasians, after all. Out of solidarity with all the Black men in my life, I never identified as "white," and I never will, as I have Black kids.

CHAPTER 3:
"D" is for Divorce

Last Mother's Day, my friend Mindy, whom I admire very much as a mother, sent me this message: "Happy Mother's Day, Gözde. Your devotion and action for your children are an inspiration." This put tears in my eyes. I felt very proud. Mindy also told me after my custody battle, "Gözde, you still did something amazing. You can provide safe space for your kids 50 % of the time." This holds true. I am the person who the kids ask questions about puberty, sex, and what they should do about their crush at school. I am their rock. After I went through and suffered through divorce, I would say "yes" if you asked me today if I would do it all over. But would I wish this on anybody? Definitely not. Multiple friends going through a hard time with their marriage asked me if they should go through with a divorce. I told them,

"Try to work it out unless you are emotionally or physically abused. If your partner is difficult right now, they will be triple-difficult during divorce."

You see a person's real face during a divorce. I tried to be kind and compassionate while getting divorced, even though my ex really tested me. One day, I blew up on my ex while meeting my son's psychiatrist. Everything I could not tell him during divorce proceedings came out. I said, "You are delusional to think you are dealing with your mental health without medical help. This destroyed our marriage. You have been blocking our son from getting the medical help he needs. You are going to make him another statistic." I resent my ex, and that sometimes comes out even with my best intentions, especially when he makes decisions around our kids without really thinking of them. I am the momma bear and will do anything to protect my kids from anybody, even if that person is their dad.

Divorce is a woman's worst nightmare. This partly stems from wanting to give our kids the best environment, so they become the best version of themselves. I was one of those women as well. I thought divorce was the furthest thing from my relationship. When it crept up on me, and I got blindsided, I was very shocked. When we were in the thick of the custody battle, and the kids were with me full time, my oldest kept asking me why he could not see his dad, and he was not coming to the house anymore. I told him, "K, I am doing what is best for you and your brothers. Please trust me in this process."

Even though I thought I did the best thing for my kids by getting out of my marriage, the sorrow gets you and makes you question if you made the right choice. When the kids ask over and over why we got divorced, it is hard to answer them and not get sad. I never mentioned to my kids about their dad's mental health issues. I just told them that their dad and I stopped loving each other romantically, and we decided to be co-parents instead. I did not want to say anything bad about their father and poison their thoughts about him. When my oldest son was 10, we were together with friends at a Turkish restaurant. He turned to me and said, "We are never going to be able to go on vacation as a family anymore."

He looked around when we were all togeth-er for a party and said, "We are together as a family again."

My heart breaks when I hear that. He was 8 when we decided to separate, and he is the only kid who probably remembers us being a family. He is so mature and well beyond his years. I hate that he had to grow up fast be-cause of the divorce. I hate that he is a child of divorce. I thought I did all the right work by finding a partner who could be a good dad and husband so my kids could learn from him. Unfortunately, we all come to marriage with our baggage and traumas. If those traumas are not dealt with and become bigger than what we can deal with, the people closest to us can become a scapegoat.

When I started this book, I did not plan on writing about my divorce. Maybe it was too hurtful for me or too private. As time went on, I realized that it might be good to talk about it not just for myself but also for other people who want to take lessons from my life.

Let me say this: If you are under 35 and reading this, I must warn you that you might not want to get married after reading this chapter. So, just skip to the next chapter.

Now that I am done with divorce, I can tell you this: if you want to be with someone long term, don't have kids with this person. There is no way of being romantically involved with someone, having kids, and not wrecking that relationship. If you have done this—congratulations, you have managed to do the impossible. I don't think it is even biologically possible to be a mom and dad and a lover simultaneously. Take it from a mom: as soon as I became a mom, my focus shifted completely to my kids. If it doesn't happen that way, I think something is wrong with you. Your body and hormones prepare you for this moment. You found a man who could be the perfect dad for your kids. As soon as you have your first baby, your focus changes completely to this little human. It is all about feeding him/her, bathing him/her, educating him/her—nothing else matters.

I know it doesn't happen to everyone, but I was one of the lucky ones: each time I had a baby, I was high on happiness for about 6 to 8 weeks. Nothing else existed for me but this little human. After three times, there is no room for someone else. If your spouse gets this and comes along for this ride—taking nothing personally—potentially, this might work. It rarely happens this way, though. I still would not trade my life for one without kids. I have wanted to be a mother since I was a little girl. I knew I was going to have multiple kids. I always thought they all would be biological kids, but, in the end, I ended up having a kid (C.) that was not biologically mine, but I loved him just as much.

Even though what I just told you is true, I could have still stayed married if my ex was mentally OK. Because as a mom, you also want your children to have the best life, and this includes a mom and a dad in harmony under the same roof. If you are not in love with this person anymore or this person is not the perfect husband, but he is an amazing dad, you stay. My ex was and is a good dad, but somehow, we lost him along the way. He increasingly lost touch with me, with the kids, and with life. He was so consumed with the trauma of growing up as a Black man in this country and his depression that we literally lost him. I still tried to be there for him and tried to salvage what was left of our family, but that wasn't enough. He started to take it out on me and turned on me—not physically, but emotionally. Then I had two choices: stay and get sucked into his deep hole or float and be there for my kids. I am sure you've guessed it: I picked the latter one.

Don't get me wrong, this was not an easy decision. It took years to get there, but one day, he did something, and then I was done. There was no going back. Shortly after we decided to separate, the COVID-19 pandemic started, so we ended up living in the same house for nine months. I have to say that nobody should be forced to live in the same house with someone that they just broke up with. It is against nature. I think we still managed to keep it OK for the most part until the end. This still took a lot of self-control to not get into fights or say something that you think they deserved. I am writing this in a hotel room, wondering how my kids are, and hoping to see them soon.

I remember that one of the things I realized while we were trying to separate was that I was in a codependent relationship. He was the damaged one I had to protect/save, but I lost myself. Of course, his turning on me was a wake-up call, but also, I also realized that if I got sick today, he would kick me to the curb and not be able to take care of me. He became one of my children, but I needed a partner!

He told me that I caused 85% of his depression. That's the exact number he gave; I think that's when I reached my limit. Of course, I didn't believe him. I thought there were two possible explanations for why he told me this. One is that he really believed it, which was worrisome. The second was that he didn't believe it, but he wanted to hurt me—which was even worse. As I tried to process this, he left our bed for good, started sleeping on the couch, and became aggressive. I will never forget this incident: I had surgery two weeks after we had this talk. After breast-feeding three kids, I had some extra breast tissue under my arms. Although they were not malignant, the doctor thought removing them was a good idea. I asked my ex if he could get me from the hospital, but he said he had a therapy session and couldn't. I said OK, I would ask the nanny then.

On the day of the surgery, I came back home with the nanny. He asked me very coldly if the surgery went OK. The next day, our nanny was off. He took care of the kids but didn't even come and ask about me, like if I needed a glass of water or anything. How cruel is that? After talking to my mom that night, I talked to him about his behavior. We were going to leave in two days to go to Atlanta for Christmas, and I asked him if he wanted me to be there at all. He said it was my decision. We talked for a while, and he said very mean things. One that hit me the most was when I asked, "Why didn't you come get me from the hospital after the surgery?" He said, "You hadn't died; why would I come to get you?"

When he told me that, I knew that this relationship was done. That was the moment!

I changed my ticket to Atlanta the next day and stayed home for three extra days. But I didn't want to be away from the kids for two weeks. When I got to Atlanta, he was very distant with me and wouldn't even look at me. I talked to his mom and told her that she would be my mom forever, but I could not be my ex's wife anymore. I said I tried my very best but could no longer continue. She told me that she understood.

Over the following months, my ex said many things that I don't know how I endured listening to. He said I was a control freak and tried to control him and his life. I kept listening and started believing what he said. I hadn't realized that I was doing it, but maybe I was. I like to control things around me, but I didn't think I was trying to control people. However, I believed that when he said it.

Ten months after the separation and two weeks after we separated, it dawned on me that my ex was the control freak. He wouldn't even let me pick out curtains for our bedroom. He didn't want curtains. There was no way to convince him. How does a professional man busy with work and family care about curtains? We were talking to a couples' therapist months before our separation, and because he was going through so much with his depression, she suggested that I make the decisions about the family and little things around the house so that he could concentrate on getting better. He agreed, and six months after that, we decided to separate, and he blamed me for being a control freak. He always questioned everything I said. He would never be OK with anything.

He also blamed me for being dismissive and judgmental. Now, I look back and see that he was the one who was dismissive and judgmental. Nothing was ever good enough for him; he always criticized everything. He told me that he was never a good enough man for me, but I always thought and told him numerous times that he was one of the smartest people I'd ever met, and I meant it. He could do almost anything if he put his mind to it, both physically and professionally. He was a biologist when I met him. Then, by educating himself, he became a software engineer and a UI engineer by reading books and working on them. His mind played tricks on him, and he thought he would get fired every couple of years. He would either change his job or department after that. Whenever he tried to go down that path, I would try to intervene and help him, but nothing would help.

I think the hardest thing in divorce is sharing the kids. Not being able to see my kids every day is one of the hardest things I have had to do in my life. That and hearing that they would rather be with their dad when you show up to see them. Your heart breaks every time. You must keep reminding yourself that this is the best decision for you and them. Nobody gets married thinking they would get divorced. I got married thinking this was for life. We would send our kids to college together, retire together, and even move back to Turkey together.

I think I finally let my ex go in my head when I discovered he had a girlfriend. This information somehow switched something in me. Maybe I realized I was just a path to him finding his real self. Maybe my codependence kept me feeling guilty about leaving him and seeing him lonely. I somehow could not move on. Of course, my heart sank when I first found out that he was dating and possibly in love. I think I held onto the idea of my ex for years. When he was dealing with depression and who knows what else and became a shell of his former self, I continued to hold onto the idea of a marriage. I increasingly did more and more physically and emotionally. I always hoped that he would become the man in my head. When he turned on me and blamed me for everything, I had no choice but to leave if I wanted to salvage any sense of myself. Maybe this was his intention, or maybe not—we will never know. I think that seeing him move on was my closure.

Before the divorce, when the marriage was on the rocks, I started seeing a therapist, a Turkish lady who was in the US for her husband's job. She'd had a baby recently, so she was mostly home and caring for her kid. She really was great with me the whole way. She was there when I was trying to pick up the pieces of what was left of me, reminding me how strong I am. It was amazing having her be a part of my journey.

I also started talking to an interesting Turkish hippy therapist through WhatsApp. He was a believer in dreams and what they meant. During our second session, I discussed a heated interaction with my ex. This happened after months of trying to take the high road, but my ex finally pushed me over the edge. The therapist started asking me a lot of questions about my ex, his family, and his mom. Afterward, he came up with an explanation: my ex was associating his mom with me, and all the things he said to me were the things that he wanted to tell her. He blamed his mom for pushing his dad out for years, and now he blamed me for pushing him out. He worried I would take the kids and run just like his mom did.

In 2020, while working with a mediator, my ex was terrible. I really thought he was trying to break me. He would say "no" to everything I asked, whether it was about finances or the kids. He couldn't look me in the eye because he had so much hatred for me. I found a piece of paper (probably addressed to his therapist) at home one day detailing how much he hated me, including our sex life. He wrote about how I was so condescending, controlling, and bad in bed. But I only took control when he couldn't do the things because he was so deeply down into depression. I took care of the kids' doctor appointments, medication (my three sons have ADHD), and following up on their diet so they don't lose weight on the ADHD medication. I got all their clothes and shoes and made sure we paid the school and the nanny. I clipped their nails and even had to ask him if I wanted him to do something that small. I did the laundry every weekend, and when I started working full-time and could not cook anymore, I found a service that covered cooking dinner for three or four nights a week.

My ex was involved in the kids' education when he wanted to be. He did most of their distance learning during the pandemic for about five or six months, which I was thankful for as I had to go to work. He bragged about it, though, and made sure to tell me every chance he got. He got their Christmas gifts every year, and the year we decided to separate, he told me I could not pick the kids' Christmas presents because I didn't know what they would like. At the end of the day, I believed that I was my kids' savior: I saved them from growing up with two parents that are depressed and lost. I saved them by saving myself.

Around Christmas 2020, when we almost signed the Marriage Settlement Agreement (MSA), I started having dreams of my ex. These dreams were from the good times, how we celebrated Christmas together and talked about the kids' presents, or when we discussed financing our new house. I was trying to make sense of it all. Maybe my brain was trying to remind me of the good times while I was at war with him. I realized that I loved him very much; even when I channeled my love to the kids, I loved him through the kids. He couldn't see this, though. He was so involved with his own trauma that he did not see how much I loved him. I was the wife, I was the husband, I was the mom, I was the dad, I was the auntie, I was the uncle, I was the stay-at-home mom, I was the provider, but that was still not enough. I think I loved him more than he could ever think of loving me.

My hippy therapist told me that we set a scenario in our childhood for us to play later in life, a theory set out by psychiatrist Eric Berne. My ex found a woman (me) to repair his mom. Our marriage was never supposed to work out; he was living the scenario he produced and lived as a little kid. That idea makes so much sense now, and he always told me that he thought he was going to end up alone. From very early on, I was the mother figure, taking care of my sister and my parents. I then took C. (my ex's nephew) under my wing. Then, I had my kids. My ex made sure that I was the perfect person to do this, and I picked up where he couldn't without complaining. I am strong and will make sure all the kids will be OK no matter what. I was playing a matriarch role with his family. They loved me and respected my opinions. His brothers thought I kept the family together.

My ex was trying to repair his dad by being the best dad he could. He even baked cookies with the kids the other day; he hasn't done anything like that in so long. He was also scared that he would be like his dad and die alone. He thought that I would take away everything and leave him penniless. My therapist said he felt like I was feeling worthless because of how my ex handled the divorce. That worthlessness also came from my childhood. My parents expected me to be a boy but had a girl instead. Growing up, I felt I was the most worthless in our household. Thinking back, that is probably why I left home, trying to escape that feeling of worthlessness. I needed to find myself. I wasn't this ugly, mediocre student who would probably not get anywhere. I had to redeem myself.

After a year of working with the mediator, my ex and I reached an impasse. I was sad because I really believed in the process of mediation. During the last four months of sessions, he was dissatisfied with everything we discussed and constantly mentioned his lawyer. He didn't want to give me the title of the house we mainly stayed in with the kids, although we agreed months ago that he would. Finally, as I thought we were about to sign the MSA, he came up with another issue. He didn't want to "nest" anymore. Nesting is a solution for divorced or separated couples where the children stay in the family house while the parents come and go. This way, the kids are more stable physically and mentally. Because I was not entirely sure of his mental state, this was the only way I could think of to ensure that the children could be safe as another adult was living in the house (our nephew). We also used to have a live-in nanny, but she left because of my ex's behavior.

My ex suddenly asking to take the kids to his house made me really worried about their safety. What also didn't help was my oldest son telling me that my ex fell asleep before they went to bed one day, and my son had to give his brothers dessert, brush their teeth, and put them to bed. This had happened before we started nesting when I was working at night and had them during the day because of the pandemic. Then, we had a nanny who would step in or call me. I would tell her to wake him up, but she wouldn't. The kids would be going crazy, running back and forth, screaming, but he would not wake up. He probably passed out. He had depression, and he was self-medicating with legal drugs. I think after years of doing this, it became an addiction. I had no choice but to get a lawyer. In about three days, I found this amazing lawyer: Michelle Harris of Harris Family Law. She totally got me right after our first fifteen-minute talk and was there with me every step of the way. When my ex shocked us and said he was taking the kids that weekend to his house, I had to squat at home and not let him take the kids. I discovered that if I let him take the kids once, I would have no case against him regarding custody because I let him take them. On the other hand, he could fall asleep around the kids before they went to bed, smoke weed since it was legal, and be a grade-C parent most of the time, and it was OK. I don't know if you see the irony in that.

When he showed up to pick up the kids, he had his phone camera and was recording me. He said that he legally should be able to see his kids. I told him that according to our verbal agreement, he could not just take the kids immediately. We should let the lawyers handle the situation. He wasn't happy, but he said goodbye to the kids and left. My lawyer and I then filed a motion saying he was self-medicating and making unilateral decisions about the kids. We got a court date about five months later.

My lawyer told me on day one that I probably could not get custody of the kids more than fifty percent of the time and prepared me for that. She suggested hiring a nanny who could go between houses. That way, the kids will have a stable person they see wherever they are.

In the first four weeks, my ex came and saw the kids for about ten to fifteen minutes every other day, standing by the door without stepping inside. He acted like there was something really bad inside the house. After a month of having the kids one hundred percent of the time, my lawyer and I tried to push his lawyer to maintain the status quo (nesting, which the kids are used to) until we found a nanny whom we would share. My ex said no to both ideas and filed an *ex parte* motion for an emergency hearing for the custody of the kids. He then started coming in and spending a little bit more time, like an hour or so, in the kids' room. That was an improvement, but the kids were still suffering. They kept asking why Daddy wasn't there anymore and they couldn't visit him at his house. His explanations also made no sense. He told the kids he needed a court order to take them places, which wasn't technically true. They missed him. My youngest son, A. (who was 4 then), cried for his Daddy every time something happened or at night. I felt like I was swimming in a swamp. I could not go forward in any way, and it seemed like every time I moved, I was sinking. I was at home two days out of five days and didn't know how long my company would let me do this. They were very understanding, but it was also an important year for the company, and they needed people to work extra—not less than normal. Around this time, I finally found a live-in nanny: Kelly. She was amazing from the beginning.

After seven weeks of hell, the court appointed a mediator from Family Court Services. She was supposed to mediate the situation and suggest to the judge how custody should go. She was great at listening to us and redirecting. She convinced my ex to consider the nanny as help and take a very slow approach to getting the kids to his place. He was not supposed to have overnights right away. There were no precautions for his weed smoking or not going to his psychiatrist on a regular basis. I could say everything on my mind, including his passing out on the kids multiple times and his being nasty to everyone at home. His problems started before the divorce, not after. He showed erratic behavior, self-medicated, and put kids in danger. I was very calm and mostly cooperative. I responded to everything that he threw my way. I still felt defeated after it all went down. Then, all we could do was wait for the court.

In this mediation session, he said one thing that really bothered me: he told her that he smoked a lot of weed during the last year and a half because our marriage was very toxic. I thought, "What the hell?" I am a quick responder, so I said that seems impossible. He had been smoking weed longer than one and a half years. But the word *toxic* was what really stuck with me the most. "Toxic," really?

Here is my interpretation of what happened: he one day woke up and had to find
a scapegoat for his feelings of low self-worth.
He found me to blame for everything. When I
didn't take it and asked for a divorce instead,
he got angry because he couldn't leave the
marriage. We were in a codependent relationship, and he was the dependent. Although I
was sad, I made peace with the situation, but
he couldn't, so he got increasingly angry and
said "no" to everything I said. He was punishing
me. He was the toxic one in our relationship.

I realized that I enabled my ex to be who
he is throughout our marriage. I didn't push
him enough to get better help when it came
to mental health. I just thought it was hard to
be a Black man, and maybe giving him a break
would help him. His not being well affects my
kids' safety and health, so I realize now that I
made a mistake. I hoped that the help of the
court and legal system and being unable to
take the kids to his own house without consent would make him reconsider and reevalu-
ate. We need more Black men not to get lost. I
know he is lost. He thinks I am the enemy, but
I hope he will realize one day that I am doing

the best for the kids and him. I finally chose the kids over him—I hadn't always done that in my marriage.

Finally, we had the court date on March 18, 2021, fifteen months after separation. It was a cliffhanger. We had received the report from the Family Court Services a week before. My lawyer replied that we agreed with what the mediator said with minor adjustments. We hadn't heard anything from my ex. It seemed like his lawyer didn't know much either. We showed up to the court, not knowing what would happen. My lawyer had said not to expect much from this first hearing and that we might get another date for the continuance. We showed up on a video call (it was still the pandemic) and were called quickly after. The judge was a powerful woman who would not take any crap from anybody. She saw right through my ex and his lawyer, didn't let any of their arguments stand. It was a real "me too" movement moment. She even said, "This woman makes way less than the man and even took a 5-year break so she could support his career, so please stop this nonsense." Most importantly, my ex was ordered not to smoke weed or drink alcohol 48 hours before getting the kids. This was huge.

We also agreed to meet again in six months to review his parenting and our custody plan. We had to share the nanny that I had already hired. We were only to use a co-parenting app for any kind of communication and correspondence. This app was to be monitored by the court when necessary. The judge also ruled that my ex was to pay almost full-time care for the past two months that I was practically a single mom and also ordered that my ex pay most of my lawyer fees. Although it was a victory on almost all counts, I felt like I was hit by a bus at the end of the hearing. I cried uncontrollably for about half an hour, calling friends and family. I also felt bad for him even though he deserved all of it and more. One side of me, of course, still cared for him like a mother cared for her child. Maybe the codependent in me that was having a hard time letting go. I don't know.

The next day, I talked to my therapist about my feelings. I said I was feeling like an animal who came back from war, cleaning my weapons and polishing them, and then I was trying to comb my ruffled feathers as I was calming my soul. I was trying to return to that calm and patient Gözde that I loved and admired. The Gözde who fought relentlessly, who could take anybody and anything down—but that wasn't the little girl in me.

No one ever tells you this, but when you get divorced, you have to separate everything: Amazon accounts, Costco accounts, gas, and electricity. Every time he brought something up, I was pretty upset. When he asked to separate his Netflix account, I lost it. We share the Netflix account with some family and some friends abroad. I was the one who he had to leave? This bothered me, especially thinking that his kids would be watching TV half the time at my home. I called him vindictive for doing this—I found it so petty. I don't know why, but this was the part of the breakup that was hard for me. We couldn't share a Costco card now that we were divorcing. I have to pay a separate fee to get a card so that I can get stuff to feed our kids or wipe their butts. I simply didn't understand. I guess we were not a family anymore (even though they tell you that you are a family because you have kids). Everything had to be individualistic (the American way): get your own accounts for everything and never share with anybody.

We were still trying to settle things during a period after the court hearing but before we signed the papers. During this time, my ex and I continued to disagree. He started to bully the nanny. After two or three incidents of pissing her off, she shut down. I got along well with her, so I think that's why she stuck with us for a while. My lawyer was very surprised that he continued to be difficult. Then, the nanny got sick with cancer, and we had to let her go. I know what you are thinking: is this really true? Could this all have happened? Yes, it has. Sometimes, I have to remind myself of everything repeatedly because I can't remember how we got here.

During this time, we also started talking to a co-parenting therapist. This was an interesting interaction—my ex and I had to sit on a video call with a therapist. It was difficult to look at his face in those sessions. Our therapist was a nice Black lady who seemed to know what she was talking about. She really helped us communicate better. It was still hard to get my ex to agree because he was inflexible. They say flexibility is a good sign of mental health, but he mostly wasn't flexible. I also found out that he stopped taking his antidepressants. These were mostly helpful sessions, but my ex was very difficult. It was already hard for the kids to go back and forth in our 2-2-5-5 plan, but then we had to incorporate the holidays. This meant that when a holiday belonged to one parent that year, the kids had to get uprooted for that specific day regardless of where they were. I tried to fight this because I thought the kids' stability was the most important thing. It is OK if I don't see them on my birthday. I can see them when my time comes and celebrate with them then. Our therapist understood where I was coming from and helped to find a middle ground. I felt like because of my mediation background, I was always willing to work things out. It was very frustrating, though, because whenever I tried to find a middle ground, my ex would say "no." Apparently, he learned to say "no" to me after we separated. His inflexibility with me, the nanny, and the nephew continued to show that he was not dealing with his condition. Choose your weapon: is it good to be married to a person like that or co-parent with them? Like my therapist always says—at least I don't have to live with this person or share my life with him.

I learned that my ex wanted a solo vacation in one of these co-parenting therapy sessions. I was, of course, OK with it as I will also have to go on vacation by myself someday. I didn't know where he was going, but I thought *it better not be Hawaii.* I had begged him to go to Hawaii for many years. The answer was always "no" because we could not afford it. So, when I found out that his first vacation with his new girlfriend (before our divorce was finalized) was to Hawaii, I was totally crushed. He didn't try to hide it either. He told the kids and apparently put his pictures with his girlfriend in Hawaii on Facebook. I really thought he did it on purpose, consciously or subconsciously. This man-child was out to get me. He had no regard for his soon-to-be ex-wife and was trying to crush her. I thought of doing things to him but always chose the high road. I also didn't want to give him the satisfaction of seeing me hurt.

I sometimes think that men have no idea how much women can give in a relationship. When a woman loves, she gives so much because she has so much to give. It is hard to be on the receiving end of things as men don't have that much to give. When they cannot reciprocate, they assume the women must be fake or have bad intentions. Things are so unequal between the sexes. Women can be mothers, lovers, friends, and daughters all at the same time, and they rock. Men have a hard time with that. When they are good fathers, their relationships with their friends suffer. If they are good husbands, they are shitty dads or sons. When my ex could not keep up with me being good at everything, he tried to pull me down instead of helping me. He competed with me—he thought that was the way to go. Even after we broke up, he tried to compete with me about being a parent. What he was missing, though, was empathy.

He could not be empathetic because of his mental condition; if you can't be empathetic, you can't relate. So, when the kids had questions about race, love, and anything else in between, they came to me because they knew

I would understand them and feel what they felt.

After months of trying to get the title from my ex, I finally found a loan agent who enabled me to refinance and get the mortgage in my name only. That meant that my ex signed his name out of the title. This was a big milestone in our divorce. I felt like, after this, there was nothing else left. On the day of the signing, I was ecstatic. My ex showed up at my place, and when we were signing the papers, we sat at a table with the notary. Things were a lot more peaceful at that time. He had only a couple of things to sign. After that, the notary let him leave. The notary assured me that everything would be OK, and he signed everything we needed. He also congratulated me. I think he knew my circumstances and felt sorry for me.

Finally, the day came for finalizing the divorce (July 2022, 2.5 years after deciding to separate). I actually wrote this while waiting in a Zoom room while the lawyers talked to the judge. I thought I would get sad and go through grief as things were finalizing. But even this week, my ex made me angry. Anger takes away the sadness. I am mad at him for not letting me go through my feelings. I had been in survivor mode since the separation process began. My Cortisol levels were at an all-time high, and I still don't know how my body was able to take all this. Right before we were about to see the judge one last time—to go over the verdict and sign the papers—my lawyer warned me that it was about to get real. She said that people sometimes don't realize it, but the emotions come flooding through. As soon as she said that I started crying like crazy. I hadn't expected it. When we showed up in the Zoom room with everybody else, the judge asked my ex and me a series of questions. This almost felt like a ceremony. Instead of asking us if we wanted to spend the rest of our lives with each other, he asked if we wanted to stop being married. I answered all the questions, and when it was my ex's turn to respond, I looked up to see his reaction. My ex had a smug look on his face. I could not believe it. Even after everything he had done to me and my kids, I was sad that our marriage was ending. But seeing his face was the last proof I needed of why I had to go through what I went through.

When you marry someone, that person becomes your best friend, mom, dad, and sibling. That's why the loss is huge when you get divorced. You lose all those at once. How do you deal with that loss? After the divorce, I took time to heal and grieve and decided that I would not marry again. I will also not put anyone on a pedestal so that they become my everything because it is not necessary or healthy. I have my mom, dad, sister, friends, and kids, and I have relationships with each and every one of them. I cherish those relationships. Those relationships make me the person I am today.

I blamed my ex for not putting the kids first. How could he be selfish like that? He and his mental condition came before the kids. I guess I couldn't forgive him for that. As soon as I gave birth to each child, one by one, they always came before my own needs and feelings. I thought this was the norm. I understand now that self-care is important, but I still think that once you make the decision to have children, their needs must come first. I put my ex into that category, too. I put his needs before my own. Once he turned on me, I realized I was being a parent alone. I needed to resuscitate the part of myself that was dying and getting lost. That is when the idea of this book came about. I wanted to talk about this lost woman (me) and reach out to all the lost women (or men) out there, hoping that I could give them hope. I am so glad this happened because I think this book and my story became my savior.

All throughout my long journey through divorce, I had a very good support system from family and friends. And I encountered a lot of strangers who helped me. They went through divorce themselves and gave a helping hand to me. For example, my loan agent regularly checked on me and ended up becoming a certified divorce-lending professional because she went through a divorce herself, and my situation inspired her. The notaries who came to my house to sign the loan documents paid attention to my feelings and reassured me that everything was OK. The instructor who taught conflict coaching looked at me and said she understood me. When he found out about my divorce, my neighbor put his hand over mine and said, "I get you. I went through the same thing, and it is one of the hardest things."

I am very thankful to those strangers, and I want to pay it forward. Hopefully, publishing this book and sharing my story will help some people. Even if I can help one person, I will be grateful.

CHAPTER 4:
Mental Health

I didn't know how important mental health was until I had to deal with it day to day in my marriage. While my mom and dad had a dysfunctional marriage, they generally had good mental health. As I've written, my sister was a spirited kid (and my middle son is the same way). To this day, she talks about how when she was two years old, she kept asking my dad for a taste of his alcoholic drink. Finally, he offered her a sip, thinking she would not like the taste. However, she happened to love it. And we still laugh about it now. My sister had temper tantrums from a very early age, and no one could tell her what to do. Then, when she was 10, she mysteriously started fainting. She would feel dizzy, like her blood pressure was very low. After multiple doctor visits and tests, they figured out that she was having a hard time

71

being away from my parents at music school at a young age. This is an incredible example of how mental health might affect you physically. After talking to a therapist for a while, my sister stopped fainting.

When I moved to NYC, I started seeing a therapist. This was after my first year at graduate school. I'd been going through a bad breakup with my musician boyfriend. The therapist saw me for who I am and helped me overcome my challenges. After a while, even though the rough times were over, I still went to see her. People sometimes think that therapy is just for a crisis, but I see it as a tool that you use to maintain your mental health so that you don't have the crisis in the first place—or, if you do, you at least go through them with the least amount of damage.

Therapy helps you rewrite the narrative in your head, which is very important because sometimes the narrative is far from reality. I stopped therapy when I moved to California and didn't pick it up again until my marital problems started. Then, I found a Turkish therapist who lived in Palo Alto. Having a therapist from your own culture makes a huge difference. She really understood where I was coming from, and because she also lived in the US, she knew what it meant to be an immigrant. She showed much more compassion towards me during my divorce than my mom did. I will be forever thankful to her for all she has done for me.

When my ex started going through depressive episodes, he also saw a therapist in Palo Alto for a while. The therapist was a Black woman who was super helpful to him. She understood my ex well and even informally diagnosed his sister so he could understand his family dynamics better.

Once we left Palo Alto, he stopped therapy. After years of not seeing anybody, the stress of supporting the family (as I was home with the boys) made him seek help, and he started antidepressants when I was pregnant with our third child. He was good for a while and seemed to enjoy life more. During this time, he got a job at a tech company with a very generous six-figure salary that put all of us at ease.

But after about two years, he started having more depressive episodes. It seemed like the antidepressants were not really working for him anymore. Apparently, this kind of thing

happens, and you have to change your medication. That was right before they legalized marijuana, and before they did make pot legal, he
got a medical card and started smoking. First,
it was every couple of days or after the kids
went to bed. He liked the way he felt on weed.
I even encouraged him, as he was doing better,
and I would have given anything to see him feel
better. When someone is moody or not happy
in your household, it affects everybody. A dark
cloud hangs over your house every day, and
it is a soul-crushing experience. I tried every
way I could think of to cheer him up. I did everything in my power around the house, so he
didn't have to deal with anything other than his
job. Unfortunately, you cannot make someone
happy if they are not happy themselves. My
lawyer described me as a tap dancer who was
also trying to juggle three balls. That is what
I was doing to save my marriage while I took
care of the three boys.

   After my youngest son turned 2, I got a job
at a biotech company as a lab scientist. After
being at home for five years, returning to work
was such a rush for me. I loved working in the
lab and contributing to curing cancer every

day. It was exhilarating to start to feel like more than a mother. This really changed things between me and my ex, though. He suddenly had to do a lot more around the house, including cooking and taking care of kids after work. I was commuting, so I was gone for many hours a day every day. I think he suddenly felt alone. I did not have time to cook, so he had to do it every day. He would ask, "Why do you have to come home so late every night?"

I told him I had to prove myself again after my family break. I tried to get already-prepared meals from a Turkish lady who cooked out of her home. Later, I even got a live-in nanny, but that didn't stop his slow decline. He consistently became more and more moody. He started to use marijuana multiple times a day on top of the antidepressants. Our relationship was suffering, so I found a couple's therapist about ten months after I started work. He was very upset at first. He thought going to the therapist was a way of accepting that our marriage was over.

"How could you do this to us?" he asked.

I replied, "I am trying to give us a chance so our marriage can work."

In hindsight, I now think that a married couple should get a couple's therapist way before we did. At that late stage, all it did was show everything that was wrong. Sometimes, it can push you to end the marriage. Our therapist was a middle-aged woman who seemed to be optimistic and upbeat about getting our relationship to a healthier place. Once she realized that my ex was severely depressed, she offered to give him cognitive behavioral therapy (CBT). She continued to be our couple's therapist and my ex's individual therapist at the same time. I didn't know it at the time, but this was ethically wrong—she should have done one or the other.

Not only did she take advantage of us financially, but what started off as innocent help from a therapist turned into the catastrophic events that led to our divorce. After one of our sessions, I even found out that she texted my ex to ask him how he was doing. This is totally unethical—she took my ex's side over mine. I think this therapist didn't like me and wanted to protect my ex from me and helped him scapegoat me for his problems and crushed our marriage. When my ex woke up one morning and blamed me for being a control freak and emasculating him, he was coached by her. When my ex lost his mind and decided unilaterally that he was going to take the kids to his house, it was because she helped him get off antidepressants. This therapist told the court that my ex was fine and there was no problem with him parenting independently. The therapist could have helped my ex get the right kind of care, but she didn't. Where would we be right now if he had the right care and medication? We will never know. I do know that the right kind of care is very important when it comes to mental health. I filed a complaint against this therapist with the Board of Psychology once the divorce was finalized. They didn't do anything in the end, but they told me that this complaint will stay in her file for three years. If they get another complaint, then they might be able to do something. I feel like I have done my part. Hopefully, the universe will take care of the rest.

Three of my boys have ADHD; one has the inattentive kind, and the other two have the hyperactive and impulsive kind. Our nephew has ADHD as well. Thinking back to my struggles at school, I probably had ADHD too. I had diffi-culty concentrating in class and was daydream-ing all day. I was not good at test taking, but I never got diagnosed. I don't think there was such a thing as ADHD when I was growing up. My oldest son has the same symptoms. When our nephew was first diagnosed, we tried to change his diet and use behavioral treatments. Nothing really helped until we gave him some stimulant medicine. The difference was like night and day. Sometimes, it is just a chemical imbalance.

With my boys, I knew what to do, and they went on medication right after they were diag-nosed. It's not easy because stimulant medica-tion has some severe side effects on appetite and sleep. My oldest son's Body Mass Index (BMI) got so low that we had to stop the treat-ment. It took years to find the right combination of a non-stimulant, stimulant, and sleep medi-cine to keep him feeling somewhat normal.

My middle son (who has hyperactive ADHD), on the other hand, tolerated the medi-cine really well. He has been on a high dose daily, including on the weekends. His behav-ior is difficult to tolerate otherwise. He is so impulsive that he tells me he hates me all the time, torments his brothers, and gets lost everywhere we go, like in the supermarkets and other public places. I haven't had to call the police yet, but I came close many times. One day, we were on a beach in Half Moon Bay, and when it was time to leave, he just walked off. He was 6 at the time. I am so used to it that I don't worry so much anymore. I slowly started looking for him and asked some people along the way.

One dad was so empathetic. He said, "You must be going out of your mind."

"Not yet. My son does this on a regular basis," I replied.

I'll never forget his expression. Once my son was on stimulant medication, he became quiet and very cooperative. We still get to experience that spirited boy in the mornings and at night, though, when the medication wears off. He had been so hyperactive that he was not able to sit still in class. Once he was on medication, he finally started reading in first grade. I think my boys are very smart, and they will do great things, but if they weren't diagnosed and treated the right way, it might have taken them years to get on track.

My middle son started having behavioral issues soon after he started second grade. He did Zoom schooling for half of his kindergarten year and then in first grade because of the pandemic. Even though he did well at home on medication, he started showing really alarming behavior at school. One day, he took off from school and just started running. They barely caught him at the outside door. Then, he would hit kids, have tantrums, and even hit teachers. He was out of control. One day, he ran so fast out of the school that a car had to block him to stop him from going further.

I didn't know what was happening. He would get out of control at home once in a while, but it was rare. On medication, he was an angel at home, but he would get triggered at school. I think he also started having social anxiety, and the other kids started seeing him out of control and did not want to play with him. This broke my heart.

While I was trying to get care for my son medically, psychologically, and educationally, I had to deal with my ex. Every step I wanted to take by talking to people who knew about this kind of protocol, he would stall, ask many questions, and try to undermine me. That was exhausting. I suggested we go to another psychiatrist, and my ex said "no" and did not give his consent for me to go. Even though we did not get much help from Kaiser with mental health, he wanted to stick with it.

Kaiser is an HMO (Health Maintenance Organization) with a closed network of providers. Kaiser Permanente service areas include all or parts of California, Colorado, Georgia, Hawaii, Maryland, Oregon, Virginia, Washington, and Washington, D.C. Kaiser is great when you have no specialized disorder, and you just need regular checkups. The mental health department of Kaiser was useless, though, as they did not offer any extra help and shut down any other treatments. We already had experienced their uselessness when my ex had a hard time before. They would not accept you for urgent situations. I discovered that we might need a special education lawyer/advocate to help my son. My ex said he wasn't interested. I had to deal with a mental health patient (my ex) to figure out my kid's mental issues—it was impossible.

Right in the middle of it all, I had to deal with Gray, the man I was dating at the time. I met him right after the separation; he was my rock. He just got a new job and traveled to Turkey (out of all places, he was not Turkish) for almost two weeks. When he came back, he was delusional. He called me and said that he was not safe and there were some entities out there to get him. As soon as he said that I knew something was off. I drove to get him with my friend. There, he had a high school friend who he had called earlier. We were able to convince him to go to a hospital to get psychiatric help. At the ER, they took him in and then they transferred him to a psychiatric hospital the next day. No one knew what was happening or what triggered this. I talked to his ex-wife and his father, who both said this had never happened before.

The first day, I was super functional, like I always am, going through the motions. Someone had to do it, and Gray needed me as his ally. Once, he was at the place where he needed to be, and there was nothing else to do but wait, then it started hitting me. I was trying to make sense of what the universe was trying to show me. This is what I wanted with my ex. I wanted my ex to get help, and he never would. Now with Gray, I was experiencing something completely different. He was willing to get help and didn't even think twice about going along with what was provided to him.

Gray was a daily marijuana user for twenty years, and when he went to Turkey, he had to take a break because it is not legal there. That withdrawal, plus a multitude of other stressors, somehow seemed to put him into a delusional psychotic state. It turns out this is a phenomenon that happens in people who are dependent on marijuana. This dependence is not necessarily a chemical dependence but certainly is a psychological one. I think some people prone to certain mental problems get addicted to marijuana and start self-medicating that way.

I would not have made sense of all this if something similar hadn't happened before. It reminded me of a family trip about two years prior. That was my last time in Turkey (2019) with my ex and the kids. As soon as we got to Turkey, my ex was so depressed that he could not leave our bedroom. He was not able to smoke marijuana in Turkey since it was illegal there—and that caused him to decline. I would walk into the bedroom to find him staring at the ceiling fan for hours. When he was able to get out of the room, he was not happy. He got so bad that I begged him to go back to the US and admit himself to a hospital. He didn't do it, and we all came back after four weeks in Turkey. He went back to marijuana like nothing happened. Two months after that, we made the decision to separate. I think going cold turkey with marijuana caused him to have an episode that finally ended our marriage.

The reason I did not walk out on Gray was how he responded to the whole situation. He didn't even bat an eye about going to the ER or being admitted there with the 5150-hold process, which means you are held involuntarily for seventy-two hours.

How could I leave him when he was willing to get help? My son has mental issues, too, and if he is doing everything he can, his future partner should accept him for who he is. The pandemic showed that most of us are struggling with some mental health challenges. What you have is not important as long as you are willing to address it.

After Gray became more stable, my middle son had more issues at school. One day, it was so bad that the school called the police. As a parent, imagine getting that phone call! The secretary said that my son was so out of control that they had to call the police for his own safety. I could hear my son screaming in the background. I talked to the police officer briefly. As soon as I got off the phone, I started crying like crazy. I called my ex, as it was his day with the kids. He was on his way to get my son, and his voice turned very calm as soon as he heard my crying voice. He said he would get back to me as soon as he knew more.

While I was waiting, I decided to get functional. This is how I deal with stress: I try to find solutions as quickly as possible. I called a special education advocate and explained the situation. She referred me to a lawyer. She also helped me to write a letter to the school asking for a functional behavioral test and one-on-one aid until the situation was resolved. She told me this would help keep him from getting expelled. Then, I talked to my ex, and we finally agreed on getting a different psychiatrist for my son. My ex only changed his mind because he was scared by the police. We also talked about getting an individual therapist for my son and a family therapist. We had at least a plan for the future, so I started to feel better. We also had a meeting with the school and learned that it is standard protocol to call the police in case the student doesn't calm down and has to go to the hospital.

Within a month or so, we were able to get an appointment for him at an institute that specializes in neurophysiological assessment for kids. He was seen by a psychiatrist as we filled out forms and talked to the psychiatrist. My son was diagnosed with ADHD (attention deficit and hyperactivity disorder) and possibly ODD (oppositional defiant disorder) and some unspecified behavioral issues. In the end, the psychiatrist gave us the option of trying another medicine (a mood stabilizer and antipsychotic) along with the medicine that he had already been on. As soon as medication came up, my ex started backtracking and saying that our son did not need this medicine. My ex wanted to write to the doctors at Kaiser to ask their opinion. He was backtracking because the medicine was an antipsychotic, and he was triggered by this name. I was very firm with him and said that I did not consent to him going back to Kaiser and filed a motion for sole legal custody. We went through weeks and weeks of fighting as my son's problems at school escalated. One day, he even threatened to kill himself by putting a tie around his neck and pulling it. I don't think that he was going to go through with it, but it was his way of saying, "Mommy, I need help." Do you know how hard it is to try to help your kid, but you can't? It is one of the hardest feelings in the world to deal with. Finally, we had a mediation session at the Family Court Services.

The mediator was the same person we talked to a year ago. She was a little traditional in her views but seemed to understand my struggles with my ex. My ex showed up to the meeting saying that he was open to other medication, so I was livid. I told him that he took too long to respond to his son's struggles. The mediator agreed with me and told him the same thing. My ex called me a liar, and he told the mediator that I was abusive. I could not believe my ears. I was told not to use that kind of language by my lawyer as it gets us nowhere, but he was using it against me. After two hours of back and forth, I was able to convince the mediator to talk to our co-parenting therapist. I hoped that our therapist knew enough to tell the mediator how much I was struggling to co-parent with my ex. The mediator seemed to think that getting sole legal custody of all my kids would be difficult, but maybe I could get custody of my middle son. The only good thing that happened after the mediation session was that we started my son on the mood stabilizer through Kaiser. (Kaiser was the mediator's suggestion.) I had to go through all this and spend all that money on a private psychiatrist and a lawyer just for my ex to agree. This was not co-parenting.

After a month of waiting, the mediator's report came and said we should continue to share legal custody. I was distraught, and, at first, I couldn't believe it. It turns out the California county that we lived in is very big on giving second chances to Black men. I think, overall, that seems like a great idea as we are in the era of discrimination and systemic racism, but in my case, this decision was affecting the health and overall well-being of my children.

We still had a court date to show up before a judge for legal custody, so my lawyer and I still prepared extensively to make sure they heard my problems with my ex being oppositional to every suggestion I brought up.

Five days before our legal custody court date, we heard that our court date was postponed for three weeks—I was so disappointed. Because of COVID-19, the court had been meeting via video conferencing. But because our date has changed, we were going to be in person for that meeting. One part of me thought it was a good thing that the judge was going to see us in person. Maybe seeing me, as a concerned mom, would change his mind.

My son, on the other hand, was doing much better at school. He was still having some outbursts but had good days as well. Unfortunately, he started having nosebleeds as a side effect of his mood stabilizer—apparently, this is a rare side effect of the medicine. With Kaiser's guidance, we tried to switch from this medicine to something else. Kaiser handled our situation so unprofessionally that my son ended up having two terrible days at school, including talking about killing himself yet again. I ended up taking him to the ER where our five-hour visit was better than our experience with Kaiser Mental Health. A psychiatric nurse came and talked to my son, asking a lot of questions. They just realized that his medication dosage was all wrong for him and briefly thought of sending him to an institution for a couple of days. I was even open to that—I just wanted my son to be better. In the end, they sent us home with some medication changes and we kept my son home until he stabilized.

When the school year ended, the district suggested a NPS (non-public school) option for him. In this kind of setting, he would be getting behavioral interventions in small class-rooms along with academics. I was very hap-py to hear that option as my ex and I were at the end of our ropes about getting calls from school almost every day. I could never get sole legal custody in the end, as the divorce judge forced my hand. He said he would not approve the divorce if I didn't drop the motion. The judge also suggested that we get a parental coordinator who helps us make difficult de-cisions. This person acts like a private judge and makes decisions for the well-being of the children. When even celebrities like Angelina Jolie and Kim Kardashian—who had all the best lawyers—were not able to get more than half-custody of their children in California goes to show how lenient this state is. I have friends in other states, and they tell me that when there is substance abuse or mental health issues, those states will give the kids to the stable parent.

Looking back now, I think dealing with my ex, my son, and Gray was my struggle and test in life. I believe that everybody is born with a test or karma they have to face. I have been a very "normal," "tough" type of woman who didn't really understand very much about emotions. When I got sexually assaulted at a young age, I was very taken aback but didn't let myself drown in it. I tried to forgive the person. When I got divorced, I considered myself lucky that at least I had the means to be able to get divorced. All those things that you don't process. though, usually come back to hurt you.

I also learned that traumas from our family and childhood are very important things to deal with. I worked with a friend, Sinan, who trained as a Neuro Format specialist. This is a specialized therapy that uses techniques such as EFT (Emotional Freedom Technique) and NLP (Natural Language Processing). When you have traumas, triggers can make your brain re-live them again and again. Neuro Format tries to help your brain get unstuck. When Sinan worked with me, he would talk with me to bring up the trauma. Once I started getting emotional and crying, he would tap my head and my collarbone near the thymus. These taps would help erase the bad feelings associated with the trauma. Once successful, those memories will not make you feel pain or bring you sadness anymore.

I have worked with him about some childhood trauma and the biggest trauma I have had thus far: the divorce. Even after a session or two, I started feeling compassion for my ex. I stopped getting triggered every time my ex messaged me.

After two or three years of hell, I also went through burnout at work. There was a reorganization and my whole team and manager changed. That was brutal, and I think I was at the end of my rope when it came to resilience. I remember one day driving to work, feeling so empty. I was listening to ocean waves in the car and trying to calm myself down. I felt so depleted and all of a sudden, for the first time in my life, I thought of possibly taking antidepressants. I have never been on them before and never thought about taking them. But I was at a point where I needed help. I was already doing therapy every week and meditation to ground myself. I have been living in "survival mode" for too long and needed to get out of it. By the time I found a psychiatrist and started talking about it, things crumbled with Gray, and we broke up. I will get into the details later, but that put me in an even worse depressive mode. On top of that, trying to find the right antidepressant took a while. I was already on some type of low dose of antidepressants to prevent my migraines, so I could not use the same kind. The other kind that the doctor put me on made me agitated, and I ended up having anxiety attacks.

Needless to say, psychiatry isn't just taking the magic pill, and you are better the next day. It is work and takes a while to find the right medication. Even if the medication is right, it takes a couple of weeks to get the healing effect, and antidepressants may make you worse before they make you better. To power through those weeks was hard. But one day, I woke up energized and happy. Everything made sense, and I started not dwelling on the things that I used to dwell on before. My psychiatrist and I talked about possibly being on antidepressants for a year and then going off. But I am OK being on them for the rest of my life if I have to. I am openly talking about this because after preaching to my ex for so long about my son's condition and how he had to be medicated, it would be hypocritical of me not to get help when I needed it or act like I didn't need medication. Medication itself is not enough for mental health, and it is important to be mindful. I still do therapy once a week and try to meditate every day. I exercise and try not to worry about the future or dwell on the past.

One last thing that I did on the journey to heal myself is called family constellation. This is a therapeutic approach where you can break the cycles of unhappiness, addiction, patterns of failure, and illness. This method was developed by the German psychotherapist Bert Hellinger in the mid-1990s.

According to the Good Therapy website, family constellation works as follows: There is the seeker, a person who is trying to resolve his or her family issues. As Mark Wolynn explained in his book *It Didn't Start with You*, these family issues might come from your ancestors and not always from your immediate family. I have always had this feeling of loneliness for no reason. I surround myself with people wherever I go and have a good support system. I also thought that I kept having the same pattern in my relationships and didn't know why. A facilitator is a person who manages the session and asks questions to representatives, who are people either picked by the seeker or the facilitator to represent the family members and ancestors.

Representatives are called one by one to the "field" where the session is held. They don't know the seeker, but the facilitator asks them to talk about their feelings and how they feel about each other in the field. This exercise is thought to illuminate the disharmony within the family, and the representatives are believed to be able to feel and experience the emotions of the person whose role they have taken on.

My family constellation session was held via Zoom. I didn't turn my camera on. I got to pick people to represent my family members by texting the facilitator. It was like watching my life as a play. First, I got to pick myself. The lady I picked had never met me. The first thing she said was how she felt "numb and tired"—the things I'd felt after the last couple of years of drama. Then, the facilitator brought in my "mom." As soon as she came into the "field," she started crying and cried for the whole session. The lady who played me told my mom not to put all the trauma onto her. My grandmother and my mother's grandmother were also brought into the "field." Those ladies were very supportive of my "mom." The lady who played me told my "mom" to please release her, she was tired of carrying her mom's pain. She said, "Mom, please carry your own pain. I have enough of my own. If we each carry our own baggage and pain, we will be fine." This is so realistic since I experienced this in my life. I tried to protect my mom all those years by hiding my dad's cheating. She is an adult, though, and I, as her kid, should not be the one carry-ing her baggage and pain.

The person who represented me as a kid said, "I grew up by myself and felt very lonely. No one has ever seen me for who I was." This is also something I discovered during therapy that my mom probably was depressed and young when I was a baby. That meant that she was absent from my life emotionally. That must be the reason why I have had an underlying feeling of loneliness at all times. I have already made piece of this situation and told my mom that I forgive and understand her.

Then my kid-self turned to the adult me and said: "Please don't forget who I am, I am still here and want to be with you." My fetus self said, "I always saw relationships as respon-sibilities. That is what I learned from my elders: You have to sacrifice yourself. But it doesn't have to be that way."

The whole session took almost two hours. What did I gain from this experience? First of all, I learned that I am not alone. I have my family and ancestors supporting me in this life. Second, I learned that I should stop car-ing about other people's baggage; everyone should carry their own baggage. Third, I have to embrace myself and protect my inner child and tend to it on a regular basis. This means being gentle and compassionate with myself. Fourth, relationships do not have to be all messy and sticky, they don't have to take all you have from you. There are relationships out there that can help you grow and flourish.

After all I have done for mental health, I think I am just starting to scratch the surface. There is lifelong work to do to stay healthy for myself and my kids. But I have already realized some amazing things on this journey: there is a girl inside of me who is my biggest fan. She adores me and is so proud of what I have accomplished so far. She tells me, "Don't be scared of being on your own, you only need yourself, and you are enough." I thought I played it safe in my life by trying to hold onto someone. They ended up holding onto me. I was the strong one. I need to be not scared, take risks, and not be afraid to fall. I am resilient, and all I need is myself. Once I can do that, my kids will see the role model I am for them: a kid with ADHD who achieves whatever she wants to!

When Gray and I met, I was right in the middle of my divorce. My ex and I had decided to separate and were already talking to a mediator. Because my ex felt like he could not just move out (in case that could be used against him in court), he was sleeping on the couch. It turned out that my ex had to stay at home for multiple months as the pandemic hit. I met Gray on a dating app after I made a comment about his cooking. Apparently, that is what made him write back to me. He wanted to meet right away. We met at a peculiar cafe on a Sunday afternoon. The cafe was half restaurant and half cafe, and people were eating lunch—we were the only ones in the cafe section. We talked and had coffee and tea. He asked me about my kids and my profession. He told me about himself. He had gotten a divorce five years prior. He made it sound like his divorce was very amicable, and it was because he and his ex-wife "grew apart." After having a relationship with him, I discovered this was not the case. He was very mature and understanding about my divorce, but he did ask me what stage I was at. I naively told him that we were working with a mediator, and it should not be too long since my ex and I agreed on most things. Gray seemed like a very chill and cool guy, and I thought he was handsome. We walked out, he hugged me, and we went our separate ways.

We tried to meet up for a proper date the week after but the COVID-19 pandemic hit! I remember the day there was an order for Shelter in Place—he was so worried about me. We had a conversation in the car on my commute. That was the beginning of a sweet friendship and love affair that flourished during the pandemic. We would constantly text each other during the day, forward each other the news, talk about our personalities, past relationships, etc. After two weeks of Shelter in Place, I had to go back to work. Because the kids had to Zoom school and my ex had to work, I would start the kids' school in the morning. Then around 3 pm, the nanny would take over so that I could go to work. Our nanny was an after-school nanny, so she could do English school by Zoom in the morning. Our nephew was home, too. It was a full house with the live-in nanny, our nephew, three kids, my ex, and I. My ex was not the easiest to live with especially after the separation. Gray was a savior in that sense, keeping me occupied, lifting my spirits.

We would watch a nice movie at the same time and talk and text. I thought it was such a romantic idea. We started with an oldie, *Dial M for Murder*. It was great watching it with him. He studied architecture in grad school and really understood design after working in the tech industry for twenty-two years. He has a special eye for visual arts and movies—seeing them through his eyes was amazing. We continued watching movies together for a long time, even after we started seeing each other in person. We texted for two months before we even considered seeing each other in person. This really gave us time to get to know each other before we started our relationship, which was good. On the other hand, it was bad because I had feelings for him before we met in person. That meant that my eyes weren't really open when we actually saw each other. The pandemic really affected this dynamic—I would've probably realized things a lot quicker without the fantasy that was created by the distance. Now, I think it is very important to observe someone with an objective view before you actually date them. Once you have feelings, you tend to overlook things. Things seem more acceptable then, and you start romanticizing—at least I do.

Our shared love of the water got us closer. One night when we were video chatting, he told me that he lived in an RV. This was the cost-effective method he came up with after his divorce and also a way to live by the ocean. Apparently, that was a deal breaker for some women. It didn't matter to me. I thought it was a somewhat interesting, bohemian choice. During the pandemic, he had to work from home, though, and not having stable internet was kind of affecting his work. Also, there were some wildfires, and the air quality was bad. I suggested that maybe he should think about moving to an apartment. He was indecisive about it. One day, while he had his daughter for the weekend, one of his neighbors lost his mind and started shooting at random people with a gun. Gray had to lock his doors and hide his daughter at the back of the RV where the bedroom was. The crazy neighbor kept shooting at his RV and the car, but he thought it would be best to stay in the RV because if they got out, they would have been shot. The next thing they knew, they heard an explosion. The crazy guy lit the RV next door on fire. Gray and his daughter had to hide in the back bedroom on the floor. It was a very scary time for them. Gray kept texting with the RV manager and the police to see what they needed to do. Finally, they had a clearance so Gray and his daughter could run to safety. Thankfully, they were not hurt, but Gray lost his RV and car to the fire that stemmed from the man shooting a propane tank. All of a sudden, he was homeless and carless. He stayed at a hotel and with a friend for a while. I helped him find an apartment, and we found this very cute one-bedroom apartment in Foster City by the lagoon. It was central and close to shops and the gym, so he could ride his bike.

I thought he was this tall, silver fox who swept me off my feet because he could. He was a super understanding guy who was happy to listen to me even in the middle of the night, waking up from sleep. He saw this light in me that I believed I had, and he just mirrored it right back to me. I felt like a really sexy, amazing, smart, independent woman around him. He would go along with all the crazy ideas I had. He was the one who encouraged me to write. I didn't hold back like I did with my ex, and that actually made it better. He would make me playlists (like mix tapes from the old days). He loved oldie bands like Guns N' Roses and the Smiths but also included songs from present by artists like Post Malone and Dua Lipa.

Once my ex unilaterally made the decision to end the nesting and wanted to take the kids to his house without anybody present, I had to put my foot down. We had agreed in mediation that we would nest for two years. Then, we ended the mediation, found lawyers, and started a war. I had to take the kids 100% of the time until it all settled down, and that meant that my live-in relationship ended with Gray. Before it all went down, I was practically living with Gray when I was not with the children. That was 50% of the time and he only had his daughter every other weekend and that was the weekend that I was with my kids. We didn't mix the kids because we didn't have to, and that made our relationship even better (that was a mistake, as I found out later). My relationship with Gray took a hit because of all these changes. It was also the time when he lost his job and he had to be home as there was still a pandemic.

I tried to visit him in the evenings or after work to keep things going, but that wasn't enough. After a month of fighting and talking about breaking up, he finally broke up with me two weeks short of our first anniversary. It was brutal. I tried to live with it for a day or two but couldn't. I finally asked him for a break instead of a break-up. He thought about it and said, "Yes." It was going to be a real break, though. No talk, no communication. When I sent him away that night, after he brought my belongings from his place, I had a little sadness in my heart, but I also knew I had a chance to win him back. I told him that I would fight for him when I was out of this divorce hell. If I had lost him because of this hell that my ex caused, I don't know what I would have done. I believed that our love would survive this.

Our break was still hard, though, and I missed him a lot. I just kept my eyes on the prize and patiently waited for the day that we would see each other. I would never get married again but I could see spending the rest of my life with him. Something about him was so comfortable and familiar.

During our break, he rarely contacted me. I mostly answered when he wrote to me first. About a week before my court date, he sent me this song about how he was heartbroken. That apparently inspired a list of things that he missed about me. When I saw that list, my heart almost stopped. I got a heartache that physically hurt. I couldn't believe how much he was missing me.

He said,

"-- I miss your scent, day & night
-- I miss holding your hand
-- I miss your hugs on tippy toes
-- I miss your smile with upturned eyes

-- I miss making coffee at night to wake up with you
-- I miss you in sky high heels
-- I miss resting my head on your beating heart
-- I miss walking on the beach with you
-- I miss driving in your car, searching for chargers
-- I miss waking up with you
-- I miss making us dinner
-- I miss you making us brunch
-- I miss walking around the city with you looking for outdoor restaurant seating."

Finally, after about a month, we got back together. I didn't know how we were going to deal with everything. Things were great for a while until he had a psychotic episode. Then, Gray and I had a very rocky time. After that incident, he had become very rough around the edges. We would fight for hours about stupid things. One night, our fight got to a very unfortunate stage. He could not calm down for hours and became abusive to me. I only slept three hours the whole night. I had a dream that night about Gray being so mad that he started a fire in the apartment. Then, all of a sudden, a thought hit me: Gray's medication or dosage was not working for him. I woke up and he was sleeping. I went to work. I left work early to come and talk to him. When I told him about my dream, he was totally upset with me. He told me that he was thinking of actually going off his medicine. That was my cue. I picked up all my clothes and left the apartment. I was not going to get myself into a situation where my partner clearly needed help but was not getting it.

I thought this was the last break up, but I could not deal with being without Gray. A month later, I went back to him. We had another nine months together, and I introduced him to the kids. My oldest seemed to like him, so the three of us went to a concert together. My younger two met him just as a friend, because I didn't know how my middle son would react to me dating. On multiple occasions, my son had told me that he didn't like the idea of me dating.

Then, Gray and I finally started talking about moving in together. It seemed to make sense since we were already living together half of the time. It would be financially beneficial for both of us. I had an extra room for his daughter when she came for her weekend. I told him that he should come and spend Christmas with us and see how he felt around the kids. I had my sister and her family coming and some other friends. I thought this would be an opportunity to see my life at my house.

Gray came to my house on Christmas day. I had asked him to cook the meat, and I would take care of everything else—mostly through catering. My sister was already there, and she and Gray had met before, so they were happy to see each other. Then, more people arrived, mostly Turkish women. Out of nowhere, my oldest son asked Gray to play soccer. Normally, my son never plays sports or even asks to. I think that was his way of bonding with Gray. Gray's first reaction was, "Oh boy!" I said, "Let's go to the park and play a little and then we can come back and start cooking." When we got there, they started playing and I joined them a little. Then my sister wanted to go back home since her daughter was cold. I told Gray if he wanted to stay with my son in the park, he could, but we were going back. Gray was hesitant but ended up staying in the park with my son. Soon after we got back home, Gray and my son followed. I thought that was a little weird because he did not seem excited to play soccer with my son.

We all spent Christmas Day together and Gray slept over. I gave him a room of his own, thinking that he might need his privacy, and I slept in the kids' room. The next day, I had to go to work and told Gray he could stay with everyone if he wanted. I left, and apparently, he left right afterward. I texted him, asking what had happened. I jokingly asked if it was too much for him to spend time with my family. He said, "It was too much for me. I came home so I could take a break." That was a big warning sign. He had been at my house for not even twenty-four hours.

The next morning, my sister told me that she was triggered by Gray because he reminded her of our 2019 summer with my ex-husband. She said that Gray seemed depressed and did not want to do anything with them or the kids. My sister has been very protective of me since the divorce. My sister's husband, Antonio, also told me his worries, and he said that I needed a break from drama.

I still did not break up with Gray, but I gave him all the feedback from my family. I think I wanted to give him a chance. He first took it well and said that he wanted to grow as a partner. We talked to his psychiatrist, and he changed his medication. He seemed to be doing better.

Gray sometimes hinted that he was happy the way things were, though. I was not sure what he meant by that. I told him that once you talk about something in a relationship, you can't just take it back. After a couple of weeks, we started talking one night. He told me that he loved me, and he did not want to lose me. He said, "I will more than likely move in with you," I asked him if he was kidding. He said, "No." I said, "You are not really committing to me, you know that, right? Plus, how can I move in with you when you have not bonded with my kids? You have no interest in spending extra time with them, so you get used to them." He said, "Why would I do that? I need time to myself." He then got upset and went to his room to lie down. He thought I had shot him down. In his mind, he made a big gesture to me, and I didn't accept it. He finally came back and said,

"We are done." After all that, I was still trying to give him a chance. I packed all my clothes, and he walked me down to my car. I asked him one last time, "Are you sure you want to do this?" He said, "Yes."

I think, after all, Gray was not able to commit to me. I believe that he loved me, but because of the trauma from his divorce and his mom, he wasn't able to commit to me. I, on the other hand, loved greatly as usual. My love comes with sacrifices. I am OK with that. I realize that that's why people don't fall in love later in life. It is not good for you. When you are younger, you heal easier.

I sent him a letter after our break-up so I could find some closure:

Hello Gray,

First of all, I would like to thank you for all you have done for me. You were the one person who helped me the most during the most difficult time in my adult life. I will forever be thankful to you for that. Also, I have other things that I feel I wanted to tell you:

1. I need an apology for stringing me along for almost three years the way you did. You let me fall in love with you and believe in a fairy tale. All the while, you had no capacity to commit.

2. I need an apology for taking away valuable time from my prime years, especially as a divorced woman. You kept me around and let me believe in a guy that you are not.

3. I need an apology because you could not commit. I am sure you didn't tell your ex-wife that you will "more than likely" get married to her. In your own words, I was a "phenomenal partner." I invested and sacrificed a lot for this relationship. I lived the relationship at 100%, giving my all (whatever was left from my children). You lived the relationship at 50% or less.

4. I need an apology for making me lose all hope in love and trust in men.

5. I need an apology for not introducing me to your daughter and making me wait for months. I felt not valued at all

because I know you introduced her to your partners in previous relationships.
6. I need an apology for not trying to bond with my kids even though you know how important they are to me.

I think that there were some early signs that Gray was not interested in a life with me and my kids, contrary to what he said. I wanted to believe that he was the right guy for me. I also did not want to be alone and go out there to find another person. I was tired and trying to work out a broken relationship seemed easier than going out there alone and possibly looking for another person. I held on to relationships just like my mom did with her marriage and tried to save them by ignoring the red flags.

After soul-searching for months after my final break up with Gray (this included talking to my therapist, astrologist, and friends, and doing family constellation therapy), I realized that there were lessons to be learned. My karma is to learn how to love myself and be self-compassionate. I have to put myself first physically and mentally. I don't need someone else to feel complete. I am already complete and have my roots down with my kids. When the time comes, the right person will come along and accept me for who I am. I fixed and strengthened my relationship with my mom, telling her that I understood why she didn't leave her marriage when I was a baby. I told her I was probably mimicking her by staying in relationships longer than necessary.

With the help of antidepressants initially lifting the gray clouds over my head (pun intended) and doing the necessary work I mentioned above, I realized I am happy alone. I have a good support system, including friends and family. I don't need a man in my life just because that is how it "should" be. After freaking out when I came home alone on a Friday night with no plans, I actually started enjoying days without anybody. I can do whatever I want—like eating in front of the TV—and have nothing to worry about. I am even going on vacation abroad by myself for the first time in my life. The house is so quiet when the kids are not there, and I feel at peace. Worrying about no one but myself has its perks and it is very grounding for a person like me who worries about everybody else all the time.

After doing all the work, I decided that it was time for me to start dating again. I signed up for online dating but was also open to friends introducing me to people. I realized quickly after I started online dating that it is a social experiment for me to see what is out there. I like talking to people and have a way of getting people to talk about themselves. People like opening up to me.

I didn't have an agenda like I needed to meet a person right away. I was happy to enjoy the journey. One of the first things I realized was that I got a lot of attention. I got many, many "likes." Apparently, that is not the case for men. They barely get likes—or matches, for that matter. I think that might stem from the inequality of the numbers of men and women in the area I live. When you both like each other, then you are a match. I was using a platform that let people message me even though we were not a match. That also opened up conversations with people I did not like.

The statistics were something like this: If I had about 100 likes, I might have had 20 matches. Out of those 20 matches, maybe 10 responded. Maybe 5 of those continued with the conversation. I refused to chase a man if he was not trying to get to know me. I even got into an argument with a guy when he asked me why I wasn't writing to him. I said I wasn't about to chase him if he wasn't going to chase me. He said, "I pay for this service, we are in 2023. I am not chasing women." This kind of mentality was not going to get me anywhere.

Out of those 5 men, I had one date with a guy, and then it didn't lead anywhere because he thought he was much older than me. I had three dates with another guy, and there was no real chemistry in the end, but I stayed friends with him. There was one guy I had really great phone chemistry with, but then that did not really continue when we saw each other. That taught me that it is good to see the person right after you match without delay. Seeing a person might show you things that you don't hear on the phone or realize by texting.

These numbers show that even though it seems like you have a lot of choices at the beginning (100), you end up with 1 or maybe 2 good candidates. Those might not be your person after all. Even though Tinder is the hook-up site, and the other apps are for relationships, there are a lot of men out there who want shallow relationships. Sifting through those and finding good men is not easy. They don't come out and tell you that. There was one guy that I really liked and thought we had good chemistry on the phone and in person. Then, he came out and said he was not ready for a relationship when we started talking about going on a second date. I am thankful that he said it then, not later, but why are you on a website talking to women if you don't want a relationship?

When I met my ex-husband almost 20 years ago, online dating was just becoming popular. I would have been open to it if I hadn't met my husband. Back then, you used to meet people in bars, parties, or at school. It was a lot easier to just to meet someone in person. I now watch some catfishing shows now where a man or a woman talks to another person for months or even years without seeing their face and then realize that the person they were talking to was someone else. I will not waste a lot of time talking to someone before meeting them in person. If someone is avoiding meeting you or video chatting with you, that might be bad news. It is easier to cut something off at the beginning than later, once you are more invested.

My experience with Gray and dating afterward showed me that there are at least three types of men out there:

1. Cheaters: These are men who cannot stay with one woman for a long period of time. They cheat and lie, hiding the facts until they get caught. When their wives leave them, they are out there being playboys.

2. Men who have some type of mental illness or personality disorder: These men can disguise themselves really well. They tell the women they meet all sorts of stories about their ex-wives and how they were the victims in their relationships.

3. Men who were in a relationship with a woman who has some type of mental illness or personality disorder. These are the types of men I should probably be dating. It is not easy to be out of a relationship like that, though, and I can

relate. They have to have done the work mentally to be able to move on from the toll of that old relationship.

I am now just out of my first round of online dating, and I can tell you that I am tired. I need a break. Just thinking back to Gray, I wanted to believe the things he said. I did not bother to fact-check them. It is easier to believe a fairy tale—that this is your person—so you don't have to go out there again. It is important not to be lazy. If you are determined to find the right person for you, you will find them. This person might not be the person for the rest of your life, but nevertheless, you can have an amazing time.

Let me reiterate that I think it is very important to be content with being alone. If you are scared of being alone, you will likely make mistakes and miss red flags. I would rather be alone than be stuck in a toxic relationship. Once you understand that, you will attract the right people.

Dating after divorce is really hard. People are hurt. They don't want to trust anybody, and they don't want to repeat their mistakes.

I believe men especially have a hard time. I've dated two divorced men who were both 50 when I was 45 or 46. I thought because they were older than me, they would be more mature. Both of them ended up hurting me. One of those men, I thought, was the reason for his own divorce—the wife left him because of him. I could totally see their dynamics in my relationship with him. The second man was the abused one. Even though he used a therapist to get out of the marriage, he didn't do enough work to heal. He was in a very defensive mode, he thought he was being attacked. People tend to underestimate how much work it takes to get over a divorce. It doesn't go away by itself. If you are one of those people who married someone who is like one of their parents (like I did), then there is a lot of work to be done. If we want to be happy and not repeat our patterns, we have to understand why there is that pattern in the first place.

In general, it is hard to meet potential dates in real life. After divorce, it is especially hard as most people are still married, and if they had stayed single until then, I would be suspicious that they had commitment issues. Like I said before, when I was dating in my 20s, I could go to a bar and meet people. I am not saying that is the best place, but you could totally do that. Everything is based on dating apps now. I think it is hard to say one app is better than the other. I've tried a lot of them, though. I remember one day, one of my friends was saying that a certain app was like going through a commercial trash bin. You had to go through so much trash to find something valuable there. She liked this other app where she met her fiance'—it was more like home trash, with a lot less to go through. I met both my boyfriends on dating websites, so I can't say it was all bad. They were both good people. Things didn't work out, but I think that was because of what I mentioned above.

There are also so many crazy people out there on dating websites. Once, I came across this guy who looked great in the pictures. He said he was from Belgium but had been in the States for many years. I thought we hit it off, being immigrants in this country and so on. We talked on a messaging app for a whole week. He refused to talk on the phone; he said he wanted to increase the anticipation. I was a little skeptical.

I asked him to record his voice and send it to me. He sent a recording, and the voice really sounded like someone from Belgium. Then, out of the blue, he mentioned how Crypto was such a great way of investing. First, I diverted the conversation. Next time, he pushed harder and told me to invest $1,000 to $5,000, and he would help me navigate it. It sounded really weird, and I told him I didn't feel comfortable talking about my finances with him before we even met in person. He got mad at me and said, "Good night."

I remembered that some people had mentioned this kind of scam on dating websites. I Googled it and found that this was a common theme. Apparently, they prey on women like me and get them to invest in scam cryptos they own. They could scam people for thousands and thousands of dollars. Sometimes, they are not even in this country, just sitting in front of their computers, messaging people from another part of the world. He would send me a good morning message, a noon message, and check on me in the evening. Maybe he wasn't even a "he," now that I think about it. He was very sensitive and knew how to talk to women.

I sent the article to him, and he acted like he was insulted. I told him to get lost. It is scary to think that there are people out there trying to prey on women's vulnerability. I did feel stupid that I fell for him as much as I did, but as my therapist said, I wasted one of his weeks as much as he wasted mine, and he could not get any money from me.

Dating isn't all bad all the time, though. I did meet several people who were actually nice. One guy was a pilot, and when we started talking, he told me he was in a polyamorous relationship. He taught me the term "ENM," or ethical non-monogamy. He was married and had multiple girlfriends, but everyone knew about each other. There were no secrets, no cheating. Even though I told him that I could not possibly join his crew, he and I shared this intense chemistry. So, I did hang out with him when I was not in a relationship. I enjoyed his company and appreciated his honesty. He was different from my dad in the sense that he accepted who he was and lived his life accordingly. He did not try to live a lie and hurt people because of that, and I really admired that.

There was one other guy who was way older—10 years—than me. Even though we had a good first date, he politely let me know that he wanted to pursue other people close to his age. He didn't lead me and string me along with false hopes for three years. I appreciate honesty as much as I give it.

CHAPTER 6:
My Career Transition

When life gives you lemons, make lemonade. That has been my mantra and life's goal. That is why, even though I was going through the most challenging years of my life, I came up with a plan to change my career. I somehow knew that these experiences happened for a reason. For example, when my son could not regulate his emotions, and we got calls from school every day, I could not tell my son to "toughen up." I needed to stay calm and understand where he was coming from. I did not want my son to become like his dad: helpless and emotionally drained. As the mom, I had to do what I could to figure out how to help my son medically, psychologically, and educationally. That was my mission, and this process made me a very empathic and compassionate person. You cannot come to me with anything that is going to knock me off my seat. I have seen almost everything and will sit with you until you feel better.

I have had a huge conflict and personal trauma with a man who at the time was my husband—a conflict that was in the end unresolvable—while at that same time developing my career towards becoming a professional mediator and a conflict coach. I can almost hear you saying, "How the heck did this happen?" Sit tight, I will tell you.

Around the time my ex and I separated, I had been working at my job for a year and a half. I had come from academia, which means I had always been in a university setting. After college, I did my master's and then PhD, and then post-doctoral studies at different universities. My original plan was to become an academic, which meant some kind of a teaching position or a research position. During my postdoctoral studies at Stanford University, I decided that academia was not for me. I loved research and mentoring, but academia was very dysfunctional. There were no checks and balances, and that meant that professors ran their labs however they wanted. They were the kings of their castles (labs). No one else had a say on how they run them. There was Human Resources (HR), but they did not have any power over professors, especially if they had tenure.

My PhD studies at NYU were amazing, and I learned a lot. I had so many good mentors, and people genuinely helped each other. My postdoctoral studies at Stanford were a totally different experience, though. Stanford University is a very cutthroat, sink-or-swim environment. I did not know this when I started. My professor put me on a project with a medical student in the lab. What I did not know at the time was that this was an attempt to push the student so that he could do a better job on the project. The student took this badly and started doing experiments behind my back. When I understood what was happening, I told the student that we needed to collaborate. I told him that "we could be co-authors on a publication," and that put him at ease. I get the student's reaction, though, because, in academia, there is only one first-author on a publication. That person gets the most recognition, and if you want to go places, you need several first-author publications. (One way to get at that problem is to have more than one first co-author.)

After the initial shock, I continued at Stanford but was not totally happy with the non-collaborative environment. But I did not want to leave either because I wanted to have a publication or two before I moved on. At some point, a postdoctoral candidate visited the lab I was in. She ended up not joining the lab because of what she heard. Our professor was furious and wanted to know what happened. I sat down with him and told him all the things that were dysfunctional in his lab. He even took notes. I said, "You cannot put people on the same projects and expect them to collaborate. If you want them to collaborate, you must give them a sense of safety. Right now, they don't feel safe."

When I left the lab, the professor took a picture of my publication, and people wrote stuff around it to say goodbye. I will never forget what the professor wrote: "Gözde, we will miss you. Don't ever change."

When I joined the workforce in the private biotech sector, I thought things would be a lot different. There is definitely a functional Human Resources (HR) and People Operations, but they can't possibly put out all the fires. At the start-up company, I was the twenty-seventh employee. They hadn't even employed anybody for the HR position yet. Most people came from academia, and that meant that certain egos clashed. We started losing good scientists. Right around then, my long-time mentor and colleague Dee Dragon joined the company. She is a kick-ass, accomplished lady who wanted to set up a good culture at the company. She had really good ideas, and I wanted to join forces with her. Dee wanted to set up meetings with everybody at the company to meet one-on-one. I told her all my ideas and how I thought we were losing talent. She and I became close very quickly. She is the one who suggested that I do a Mediation Certification with Community Boards in San Francisco. Community Boards is the longest-running non-profit public mediation organization in the United States.

According to Wikipedia, "Mediation is a structured, interactive process where an impartial third party neutrally assists disputing parties in resolving conflict through the use of specialized communication and negotiation techniques." The mediation training was four days, ten hours each day, for a total of 40 hours. The trainees worked with experienced mediators and did a lot of mock mediation. To me, mediation is magical because, at the beginning of the mediation, you don't believe that these two people will ever resolve their issues. As time goes by, with the techniques that the mediators follow, people start feeling empathy for the other person. Once empathy happens, they find their way to resolution. Unfortunately, mediation doesn't always work. Both parties must want to resolve, and that is not always the case.

Right around my certification, I was also working with a mediator for my divorce. Our mediator was a lawyer and mediator because he needed to go through the court system. He loved doing mediation after years of practicing family law. He said that everything was so much easier when the parties did mediation since the court did not interfere with our affairs. My ex and I did mediation for about a year. It probably would not have been that long if it wasn't for the pandemic. Right when we were about to sign our MSA (Marital Settlement Agreement), my ex ruined everything by changing his mind about something we had agreed on long ago. That is when we got lawyers and were in a total war zone. After spending thousands of dollars on both sides, I can say that we would have achieved most of our agreements by mediation. We would have been done a year and a half ago. My ex was hateful and pitiful, and he didn't want to mediate. He wanted me to suffer. In this case, mediation didn't work. Believe it or not, that didn't damage my faith in mediation and how it could be helpful in relationships in and out of work life.

I also ended up doing conflict coaching certification with Community Boards. Conflict Coaching is a process where you act like a soundboard for a person who is in a conflict. You help them see the conflict from another point of view and help them communicate better. This was a big hit at the company I worked for. I rarely did mediation, as people would be too hesitant to bring the person they are in conflict with to me. They would rather sit and talk it out with me and come up with a plan. Sometimes, venting was all they needed.

I love talking to people, and I really listen to them. I realized this growing up. It was almost a game for me. I wanted to know what the people's problems were. Most of the time, people are not open, and they especially don't want to open up to a stranger. I loved being able to get it out of them. It is very important to have empathy for this and be able to show that you have it.

Let me back up and analyze this (because I do this all the time). Apparently, if you grow up with a narcissistic and/or unavailable parent, you become an empath. This happened to me and my sister. When we go into an environment, we start scanning for clues about how everybody is feeling. It is almost like being a sponge for emotions. Then, the next step is to figure out if you can get it out of them and fix it. I know it sounds like a lot. This is my passion, though, and I love doing that. I already do this with my friends and family. Doing it at the workplace was a stretch. Having some certification and doing around a cause (conflict) made sense.

For people to trust me, first, I had to build relationships. My relationships are super important to me. Whether I am working side by side with people or having meetings with them, I try to build a relationship. Then, it is easier for them to say hello to you or open up a little bit more each time.

When I am in a conflict session with people, I try to listen to what they are actually trying to tell me. I try to pick up on things that they haven't told themselves. Most importantly, I give an example from my life that parallels their problems. That really resonates with people, and they don't feel alone. Even though I hid my divorce at the workplace at the beginning, I slowly opened up to people about it. When you are an open book, people feel more comfortable around you. If you have no problem talking about your issues, they will open up to you. I love gaining people's trust.

Retention is one of the most important things that a company cares about. When people leave their jobs, they rarely do that for money or a different title. People leave their jobs because of a bad relationship with a manager or teammates. We spend 80% of our lives in our jobs, and if we are miserable there, that affects our whole life. Knowing this, I think it is very important to fix relationships early on. Like my good friend, mentor, and Head of People, Dee Dragon says, when the problem comes to her, it is already too late. I started doing office hours for this purpose at my company. I called it a Mediation and Conflict Coaching Office Hours. It was mostly a place-holder and a reminder for people that I existed. Also, the new employees would stumble upon it because they thought it was a meeting they had to go to. I would introduce myself and tell them about the resource. That way, I would meet them when they first come into the company and put it in their mind that I exist.

I was able to do many things at the workplace, such as: I had numerous sessions with people who just wanted to be heard. Sometimes, just being heard is enough to work through the emotions and understand how you feel about a situation. Some people wanted help to communicate better about a certain conflict. So, we would go through the things that they are comfortable saying to their manager or colleagues. I have also done mediation. That meant that two people that were in a conflict had to be in the room. This is the least favorable situation for people as the confrontation is hard. Sometimes, it had to be done, though.

I also performed team bonding events where I played games with the team I was meeting with. This would give a really good base to talk about any issues with the team. Once people had fun and relaxed with a game, they were more open. I don't want to give away too much of my trade secrets here, but in almost all cases, the teams would start talking about the conflict in question. I would never ask them directly about it, but somehow, we would come to talk about the conflict. Sometimes, we would walk out of the meeting with a set of goals for each member that we agreed on. People felt better when there was something written down, as it seemed more solidified.

I really enjoyed doing these things, and I also liked to come up with different things to fit the needs of different people. It made me feel alive to sit with people in the same room and talk about things that were important to them. I think that this will be a full-time job for me one day. I don't exactly know what that is going to look like—maybe I will be a coach and work for a company and help them. One other option is to have my own consulting company. That way, I can help more than one company at a time. No matter what it looks like, I know in my heart that this is what I will do as a job one day.

CHAPTER 7:
Conclusion

There were several reasons why I wanted to write this book. First, I wanted to tell my story so that if there are people out there stuck in their marriages and unhappy, my story might help them change something. I am not trying to tell everyone to get a divorce at all. On the contrary, I tell people to work it out if they can, as things get harder when you get divorced. If it is not something solvable, then you can get out. My story is a testament to that. You are not alone and can always find a way out.

Second, you have to take care of the child inside first. I had to really learn this the hard way. If you don't attend to that child and live your life in a way as if your inner child doesn't exist, you are doomed to fail big time. You are here because of that little human. I grew up too quickly because of the traumas I had to go through, and I didn't attend to that child very much. I learned that once you heal that child as much as you can, she gives back immensely. I am happy that I was able to heal my inner child because she makes me the person I am today. I am unapologetic, free, happy, and beautiful inside and out because of her.

Third, past or present traumas are part of life; *you* decide what to do, and *you* decide if you want to resolve them or live with them. Since I mostly resolved my past trauma, I think I am better at encountering trauma. When it happens, I go through my feelings completely. I try not to bottle anything up. Also, I think I now give the reaction it needs. For example, if someone were to harass me or sexually exploit me, I would fight back immediately. This could be either verbally or even physically, but I would not sit still like I did when I was younger. Some people might call me defensive, but I'd rather be defensive than get hurt or let someone hurt me in that way. I think handling the trauma this way helps me not let it fester.

Fourth, I think things happened to me in life for a reason. I was supposed to get a divorce and go through all the things I had to go through. This process made me the person I am today. I think one of my purposes in life is to help people either in my personal life or in the workplace. My experiences made me an extremely empathic person, and being able to help people is satisfying in multiple ways. My biggest gift is when someone tells me that I was able to touch them somehow and make their day or life better with what I can give them.

I hope that my book reaches people and helps them in some way. I am going to make it my life's work to continue helping people, and writing this book was the start of that. I continue my education and training every day so that this could become my job one day.

WHAT IS IT TO BE A WOMAN?

What is it to be a woman?
Is it really a human?
Because it seems we're a superhuman.
We're a mom, sister, daughter, partner, and a
human.

How is it possible?
I am hurting being a woman.
But still would I have chosen to be not a woman?

....

I am crying inside
But have to be strong outside
For my kids, for myself
To be the best of self

The girl inside me is the biggest fan
Says, "You're doing good, girl, keep it up"
My mom is proud
My dad is on cloud
My sister is the best support, I am blessed

Women are survivors, I am a survivor!

Gözde Yücel

MOM (23) AND I (20 DAYS)

GÖZDE (11 MONTHS), ANKARA, TURKEY

DAD (28) AND I (2.5 YEARS)

GRANDMOTHER (50) AND I (2.5 YEARS)

MY SISTER (NEWBORN) AND I (6)

MY SISTER (3) AND I (9), GÜZELÇAMLI, TURKEY

Acknowledgements:

I would like to thank my parents for bringing me to this world and giving me life. They are the reason where I am today, they were very open-minded to the things I wanted to do.

I also want to thank my children—they are the reason why I get up in the morning. They are the loves of my life.

I want to thank my ride-or-die women friends. They were the ones who became family and helped me get up when I fell. They are (in no specific order) starting with my sister Gizem, Gül, Genia, Banu, Tülay, Semra, Sevi, Zeynep, Sinem, Mindy, Deniz, Ebru D., Ebru K., Quincy, Lisa, Seda, Dee, Natalka, and Ayşe Naz. Tülay was especially helpful during really difficult times, listening to me every day.

I am also very thankful to my mother-in-law (my ex-husband's mom) and my brother-in-law (my sister's husband) Antonio. These are great examples of how you can have a family without a blood connection.

I would like to thank Gray for encouraging me to write and looking over my writing as much as he did. I would also like to thank Dave D. for reading the whole book before it was published and giving me support about the book. I would like to help Dee Dragon for her mentorship and finding me the title of my book.

Special thanks to my therapist Başak Atmanoğlu for all she has done for me. She is the main reason why I am able to stand today after falling many times.

Big thanks to Sinan for my trauma work. His expertise in neuro formatting did wonders for me.

I want to also thank my lawyer, Michelle Harris (Harris Family Law) for taking my case and guiding me. She became my partner-in-crime in the divorce and also my therapist and good mother friend.

I would love to thank my book coach and editor, David O'Neill, for believing in me and helping me believe in myself. This book would not have been a reality without him.

Gözde Yücel, a Turkish-born cancer biologist, embarked on an extra-ordinary journey from a Turkish city to become a respected scientist in the US. With a PhD in Developmental Genetics from NYU and post-doctoral studies at Stanford, she's published numerous articles and holds patents. Residing in California, Gözde's passion extends beyond science, aiming to inspire and support others through her captivating memoir, *Kismet*.

Milton Keynes UK
Ingram Content Group UK Ltd.
UKHW010252130324
439347UK00006B/99